H. Badnall

Remarks On The Judgment Delivered In The Supreme Court

In Re Bishop Merriman Vs. Dean Williams, August 26, 1880

H. Badnall

Remarks On The Judgment Delivered In The Supreme Court
In Re Bishop Merriman Vs. Dean Williams, August 26, 1880

ISBN/EAN: 9783337112585

Printed in Europe, USA, Canada, Australia, Japan

Cover: Foto ©Suzi / pixelio.de

More available books at **www.hansebooks.com**

ERRATA.

Page 19, line 32, for *containing* read *continuing*.

Page 23, line 36-7, for *in the Chapter-house of which* read *in which*.

Page 29, line 4-5, for *represented not by the Dean alone but by its own formally elected lay delegates* read *not through the Dean alone, but by the lay-delegates whom it had helped to elect*.

Ibid., line 6, omit *as well as in that of* 1876.

Page 46, line 36-7, omit *Chapter-house*.

Page 47, line 1, for *Cathedral records* read *Diocesan records, signed by the Dean of the Cathedral as President*.

Page 96, 2nd paragraph of Attorney-General's Memo., line 10, after *for the time being* insert *for the objects or purposes of such association, such office-bearer or office-bearers for the time being*.

REMARKS

ON THE

JUDGMENT DELIVERED IN THE SUPREME COURT,

In re Bishop Merriman vs. Dean Williams.

AUGUST 26, 1880.

BY

H. BADNALL, D.D.

ARCHDEACON OF THE CAPE.

PRICE ONE SHILLING.

CAPE TOWN
SAUL SOLOMON AND CO., PRINTERS.
1880.

ADVERTISEMENT.

When the following "*Remarks, &c.*," were already in the Printer's hands, I was strongly advised to append the Chief Justice's Judgment at length. Had this, the better course, been decided on sooner, shorter extracts from the Judgment would perhaps have sufficed. I have not, I trust, taken an undue liberty in presenting the Judgment under separate headings, some of them in my own words, in order to facilitate the comparison of the Judgment with the observations offered on it. The "Notes" on the Judgment which have appeared in the Grahamstown *Church Chronicle*, I did not see until the matter of the following pages was thrown into shape, and much of it written out. It was completed in advance of the "Notes," and expresses an independent estimate of the subject with which it deals. The article in the *Guardian* of October 6 I did not see until the "*Remarks*" were all but ready for the press.

H. B.

Rondebosch, November 26, 1880.

INTRODUCTORY REMARKS.

I HOPE I am right in my persuasion that I owe no apology to any one for attempting to allay in some degree the pain and alarm which the Judgment delivered in the Supreme Court* in the case of Bishop Merriman *vs.* Dean Williams on the 26th of last August has caused to many of the best and truest members of our Church in this land. If, indeed, it were my purpose to contest with civil judges points of law pure and simple, my design would be very foolish. I should be then doing essentially the same thing that Lord Romilly's Judgment does (Bishop of Natal *vs.* Gladstone and Others) when it suggests to colonial bishops to cut the prime knot of their difficulties by throwing it on the judges of our civil courts in the colonies to decide between bishops and their clergy, or between bishops and bishops, on articles of Christian faith and doctrine. But the legal questions that arise in the course of the recent Judgment are few, and those not intricate; and even with them I am concerned rather indirectly than directly, or at least subordinately to the assumption that certain facts are proved. My principal contentions relate to matters of fact, or of history, which it is only reasonable that I should be anxious to present from the stand-point of those who have been for years a living part of them. Such anxiety cannot, I hope, be construed without evident unfairness, into an imputation on the impartiality of the judges. I am sure I may say for others, as well as for myself, that we are grateful for

---

* For a verbatim and I believe very accurate report, for which I am indebted to the Grahamstown "Church Chronicle," see Appendix A.

the candour, patience, and even kindness that characterised the hearing of the case. But the subject-matter of the dispute, together with its surroundings, was new both to judges and counsel, and no amount of industry could have possessed them, within the time at their command, with that minute acquaintance with all the facts that could alone have made oversights impossible. I address myself to my task, then, not as a complainant, but as one strong in the conviction that important parts of our case—*our* case, I say, for it is the case of the diocese of Capetown every whit as much as of that of Grahamstown—admit of a construction widely different from that which the late decision has put upon them ; and that in the interests of truth, as well as for the encouragement of many disturbed hearts and minds, I am in duty bound not to keep silence. It were needless to say more by way of preface. Only a superior court can appraise, to any practical purpose, the value of a legal decision. What redress we may be able to obtain, should the Judgment of the Supreme Court be upheld, or rather, perhaps, what redress we shall decide to *seek*, is a question for the future.

THE ORIGIN OF THE RECENT TRIAL.

The Privy Council, in June, 1863 (Long *vs.* the Bishop of Capetown), incidentally to their adjudication of that case, laid down the following principles for their own guidance, and that of all concerned :—

"The Church of England, in places where there is no church established by law, is in the same situation with any other religious body, in no better but in no worse position, and the members may adopt, as the members of any other communion may adopt, rules for enforcing discipline within their body which will be binding on those who expressly or by implication have assented to them.

"It may be further laid down that when any religious or other lawful association has not only agreed on the terms of its union, but has also constituted a tribunal to determine whether the rules of the association have been violated by any of its members or not, and what shall be the consequence of such violation, then the decision of such tribunal will be binding when it has acted within the scope of its authority, has observed such forms as the rules require, if any forms be prescribed, and, if not, has proceeded in a manner consonant with the principles of justice.

"In such cases the tribunals so constituted are not in any sense courts; they derive no authority from the Crown, they have no power of their own to enforce their sentences, they must apply for that purpose to the courts established by law, and such courts will give effect to their decisions, as they give effect to the decisions of arbitrators, whose jurisdiction rests entirely upon the agreement of the parties.

"These are the principles," their Lordships proceed to say, "upon which the courts in this country have always acted in the disputes which have arisen between members of the same religious body, not being members of the Church of England. . . . . To these principles, which are founded in good sense and justice, and established by the highest authority, we desire strictly to adhere."

In 1879 occasion unhappily arose for testing the application of the foregoing principles. In April of that year Bishop Merriman thought fit to bring to an issue a standing disagreement between Dean Williams and himself as to their respective rights over the Cathedral Church of S. George, Grahamstown, by causing the Dean to be served with a notice of his intention to preach in the Cathedral on a given Sunday morning, April 27th. The Dean,—the Bishop being present, robed, and in his place,—prevented the Bishop by omitting to give out the usual hymn before the sermon, and preaching himself. The Bishop uttered some few words of protest and left the Church. In the June following, Dean Williams was duly cited before the Diocesan Tribunal to answer for this and other alleged offences, and in August, not having appeared in person or by counsel, was adjudged to have contumaciously hindered the Bishop in the exercise of his proper episcopal functions, thereby causing scandal to the Church, and was sentenced to suspension with loss of income for one calendar month, and longer until he should submit himself. Neither recognising the sentence, nor appealing to the Metropolitan, the Dean was again cited before the Diocesan Tribunal in the ensuing November and excommunicated. This last measure was against the feelings, I believe, of all concerned in it; but was in accordance with Canon 19, Section XV., which requires that "any person against whom judgment has been given, who shall refuse to obey the sentence of any tribunal of this Church, shall be, if not sentenced to suspension or deprivation, *ipso facto* suspended; and if sentenced to suspension or deprivation, *ipso facto* excommunicated: And it shall be the duty of the Bishop or Metropolitan, as the case may be, after notice given, to pronounce sentence:"—and Bishop Merriman was advised that until he should have exhausted the ecclesiastical remedies at his command, it would not be competent for him to have recourse to the civil courts. Everything having now been done, apparently, that could be done under the rules of the local church (Canons 19 and 21 of the Canons of the Church of the Province of South Africa) to maintain discipline, application was finally made to the Supreme Court, in order that effect might be given to the decisions of the Diocesan Tribunal, in accordance with the terms used by the Privy Council as above recited, and the rights of the Bishop of Grahamstown in relation to the Cathedral Church, and as involved in the proceedings taken by him against the Dean, vindicated. We next come to the Judgment of the Supreme Court.

THE ISSUES TO BE DECIDED.

These do not appear to have been presented in the pleadings with the distinctness that the Chief Justice could have desired. Mr. Justice Smith "entertained great doubts" as to whether "the rights of the plaintiff and of the Church of South Africa to property granted for ecclesiastical purposes in connection with the Church of England" could be discussed in this case. But at any rate, the Chief Justice was clear that " the real subject of contention between the parties was the legal *status* of the plaintiff as well as the defendant in respect of the Cathedral Church of Grahamstown, under, as well as independently of, the decisions of the Diocesan Tribunal." Undoubtedly the contention raised by

Bishop Merriman did relate to his right as Bishop to use the Cathedral, and officiate in it, and to prevent the Dean from using it, as Dean or Rector, while he was under a prohibition of the Diocesan Tribunal. Out of this contention four questions arise : " First,—What are the rights of the plaintiff, as a Bishop of the Church of the Province of South Africa, in relation to the Church of S. George ? In the second place,—What are the rights of the defendant, in respect of the same church as Rector and Dean ? Thirdly,—Did the defendant, by his acts or conduct, confer on the plaintiff any rights capable of being enforced in this action, which but for such acts or conduct the plaintiff would not have enjoyed ? Fourthly,—Are the respective rights of the parties in any way affected by the decisions of the Diocesan Court ?"

I. WHAT ARE THE PLAINTIFF'S RIGHTS AS A BISHOP OF THE CHURCH OF THE PROVINCE OF SOUTH AFRICA?

In other words—is Bishop Merriman the Bishop of Grahamstown for the time being? The Judgment declares that he is not ; and for two reasons,—first, because he is not Bishop Cotterill's lawful successor in the See under letters patent ; secondly, because, even if he were Bishop Cotterill's successor, he has cut himself off from the Church of England by the part taken by him in the Provincial Synod of 1870. I will take these two points in order, making my remarks as I proceed.

In 1853 the Diocese of Capetown, which originally comprised the whole of the Cape Colony and its dependencies, was divided, with Bishop Gray's consent and coöperation, into the three separate Dioceses of Capetown, Grahamstown, and Natal.

In November of that year Bishop Armstrong was consecrated by the Archbishop of Canterbury first Bishop of Grahamstown under letters patent, and in 1856, on his death, was succeeded by Bishop Cotterill, also under letters patent. Those letters patent purport to ordain and constitute—the Chief Justice says they " undoubtedly" do " ordain and constitute—the City of Grahamstown to be a Bishop's See, and the Church of S. George to be the Cathedral Church and See of Bishop Armstrong and his successors, Bishops of Grahamstown." Bishop Cotterill's letters patent are in the same terms. They also lay down " in what manner and by what process their successors are to be appointed." They are to be " named and appointed" by the Crown, " and by the Archbishop of Canterbury canonically ordained and consecrated, according to the form of the United Church of England and Ireland." " Now, it is admitted," proceeds the Chief Justice, "that the plaintiff has neither been named and appointed by the Crown, nor ordained and consecrated by the Archbishop of Canterbury ; but it is argued that, inasmuch as the Crown had, before the election and consecration of the plaintiff, discontinued the practice of issuing letters patent for the appointment of bishops in colonies possessing representative institutions, the vacancy caused by resignation of Bishop Cotterill could only be filled by means of a local election and consecration. This argument affords a very good ground for respectfully requesting the Crown to appoint a Bishop for Grahamstown and issue a licence for his consecration by the Archbishop of Canterbury, but it does not in any way strengthen the plaintiff's title under the letters patent. No such application seems to have been made to the Crown by the authorities of the Church of South Africa, nor do I see how it could have been made consistently with the canons of that Church, even assuming that the Crown would be willing to accede to the request. It has been assumed throughout the argument that the Crown would not accede to such a request; but it is by no means clear to me that the Crown has ever declared its irrevocable intention no longer to appoint Bishops for this Colony. It may well be that the Crown will not hereafter issue letters patent for the establishment of new bishoprics in colonies possessing representative institutions; but it does not follow that the Crown would refuse, upon representation made from the proper quarter, to nominate successors to bishops appointed under letters patent, which reserve this power to the Crown. At all events there is nothing in law to prevent the Crown even now at the eleventh hour from naming and appointing some other person than the plaintiff to be the Bishop of Grahamstown, and if a person so appointed were ordained and consecrated by the Archbishop of Canterbury, his title in respect of the Cathedral—so far as the existing letters patent are concerned,—would be complete."

Two grave questions here arise: the one, did these letters patent carry with them the quasi-legislative powers which they purported to carry? "The plaintiff does not deny the right of the Crown," the Chief Justice argues, "to create the body corporate known as the Lord Bishop of Grahamstown, and to constitute him and his successors to be a perpetual corporation; but if the letters patent were valid to create a perpetual corporation, they must have been equally valid to regulate the course of succession." Was it so? Admitting, for argument's sake, that the letters patent could do the one thing, could they therefore do the other? The other question relates to the actual history of the withdrawal of the letters patent, and is equally material to the main inquiry.

THE LEGAL VALUE OF THE LETTERS PATENT.

First, then, as to the validity and virtues of the letters patent. Now, it is remarkable that throughout the careful and elaborate Judgment under review, the Chief Justice, among all his numerous citations from other Judgments, never once cites that of the Privy Council in the matter of the Bishop of Natal. He does, it is true, cite a subsequent Judgment of the Privy Council (Bishop of Capetown *vs.* Bishop of Natal), in which reference is made to the case of the Bishop of Natal,—Lord Westbury's Judgment, as it is often called,—as showing that " the letters patent were not wholly void." The Judgment itself, I think I am correct in saying, he never quotes. Whether the omission is material will appear as I proceed.

It will be borne in mind that the Privy Council (Long *vs.* the Bishop of Capetown) had previously declared " that the letters patent of 1853, being issued after a Constitutional Government had been established in the Cape of Good Hope, were ineffectual to create any jurisdiction, ecclesiastical or civil, within the Colony, even if it were within the intention of the letters patent to create such jurisdiction, which we think doubtful." But this language would appear to fall very far short of that adopted by their Lordships *in re* The Bishop of Natal. In this Judgment they say, " Three principal questions arise, and have been argued before us : 1st. Were the letters patent of the 8th December, 1853, by which Dr. Gray was appointed Metropolitan, and a Metropolitan See or Province was expressed to be created, valid and good in law ? 2nd. Supposing the ecclesiastical relation of Metropolitan and Suffragan to have been created, was the grant of coercive authority and jurisdiction expressed by the letters patent to be thereby made to the Metropolitan valid and good in law? 3rd. Can the oath of canonical obedience taken by the appellant to the Bishop of Capetown, and his consent to accept his See as part of the Metropolitan Province of Capetown, confer any jurisdiction or authority on the Bishop of Capetown by which this sentence of deprivation of the Bishopric of Natal can be supported?

"With respect to the first question, we apprehend it to be clear, upon principle, that after the establishment of an independent Legislature in the settlements of the Cape of Good Hope and Natal, there was no power in the Crown by virtue of its prerogative (for these letters patent were not granted under the provisions of any statute) to establish a metropolitan see or province, or to create an ecclesiastical corporation, whose status, rights, and authority the Colony could be required to recognise.

"After a Colony or settlement has received legislative institutions, the Crown (subject to the special provisions of any Act of Parliament) stands in the same relation to that Colony or settlement as it does to the United Kingdom.

"It may be true that the Crown, as legal head of the Church, has a right to command the consecration of a bishop, but it has no power to assign him any diocese, or give him any sphere of action within the United Kingdom. The United Church of England and Ireland is not a part of the constitution in any colonial settlement; nor can its authorities, or those who bear office in it, claim to be recognised by the law of the Colony, otherwise than as the members of a voluntary association."

The Judgment then goes into the learning of the subject to show that "the course which legislation has taken," for the establishment of bishoprics abroad and at home, "is a strong proof of the correctness of these conclusions. . . . . . It is true," add their Lordships, "that it has been the practice, for many years, to insert in letters patent creating colonial bishoprics clauses which purport to confer ecclesiastical jurisdiction; but the forms of such letters patent were probably taken by the official persons who prepared them from the original forms used in the letters patent appointing the East Indian Bishops, without adverting to the fact that such last-mentioned letters patent were granted under the provisions of an Act of Parliament.

"We therefore arrive at the conclusion that although in a Crown Colony, properly so-called, or in cases where the letters patent are made in pursuance of the authority of an Act of Parliament, a Bishopric may be constituted and ecclesiastical jurisdiction conferred by the sole authority of the Crown, yet that the letters patent of the Crown will not have any such effect or operation in a Colony or settlement which is possessed of an independent Legislature.

"The same reasoning is of course decisive of the second question . . . . . It is a settled constitutional principle, or rule of law, that although the Crown may by its prerogative establish courts to proceed according to the common law, yet that it cannot create any new court to administer any other law . . . It cannot be said that any ecclesiastical tribunal or jurisdiction is required in any Colony or settlement where there is no established Church, and in the case of a settled Colony the ecclesiastical law of England cannot, for the same reason, be treated as part of the law which the settlers carried with them from the mother country."

The treatment of the third question is necessarily in keeping with that of the two questions preceding. This Judgment, as I shall show presently, has been

generally accepted as decisive. It may be admitted that in this and in the Rolls' Judgment together there are "*dicta* which"—to quote Professor Mountague Bernard,—"taken in their plain grammatical sense, seem to militate against each other, and can with difficulty be reduced, or tortured, into harmony by the most skilful master of language."*
But the fact that ever since the Judgment in the matter of the Bishop of Natal was delivered, the Imperial Government has scrupulously conformed to it, is, practically, evidence that it decided the law once and for ever. Even if we concede that the letters patent of 1853 are "not wholly void";† admitting them to be effectual to create *some sort* of corporation,—they are certainly void in law as purporting to confer jurisdiction; they cannot " create an ecclesiastical corporation whose status, rights, and authority the Colony"—or, it may therefore safely be added, any section of the Colony,—" could be required to recognise;" they cannot even, where the Crown may have rightfully ordered or allowed the consecration of a bishop, "assign him any diocese, or give him any sphere of action." Why then should they be valid as purporting to lodge the right of

---

* Remarks on some late Decisions respecting the Colonial Church, by Mountague Bernard, M.A. Chichele Professor of International Law and Diplomacy in the University of Oxford.

† The Chief Justice cites a judgment of the Privy Council (Bishop of Cape Town *vs.* Bishop of Natal) as proving that the letters patent were " not wholly void"; and that the second letters patent of the Bishop of Cape Town of 1853, and those of the Bishop of Natal, both created corporations capable of taking an estate under a grant from the Crown. But it is noticeable that that judgment is founded not on the letters patent alone, but on a series of equitable considerations grounded in common sense, and on the circumstances of the case generally, it being an inference from all these various and combined considerations "that the effect of the grant and the plaintiff's letters patent of 1853 was at least to give the plaintiff (the Bishop of Natal) the right of access to the church, the right to officiate there as Bishop, and the right to perform there all the religious services which are or ought to be performed by a bishop in a cathedral consistently with the laws and usages of the Church of England, so far as the same are applicable to the Church and Colony in question."

nomination and appointment with the Crown, and to make consecration by the Archbishop of Canterbury imperative, when it is expressly declared that they cannot give him appellate jurisdiction? "It would surely be an absurd proposition,"—to quote Professor Bernard again (Remarks, pp. 23-4)—" to say that the Crown can have legal jurisdiction over a bishop, as such, in a place where a bishop, as such, is an officer unknown to the law. The power of appointing a bishop stands, of course, on wholly different ground from that of appointing those civil officers who are necessary for the transaction of public business and the administration of justice in a Colony, and whom the Crown, as head of the Executive Government throughout the Empire, is authorised to appoint by warrant wherever their services are required. A bishop, unless he be a bishop of a church by law established, is no more a public functionary than a Baptist minister is; and he is not a public functionary within a Colony unless the church be established by law within the Colony."

WHY THE LETTERS PATENT WERE DROPPED.

But this subject receives further elucidation from the examination of the next question, namely, why the letters patent were dropped. They ceased to be issued, not because the Colonial Church failed in its duty to the Crown; nor because we made canons to shut out letters patent; but because, as it became gradually clearer that the letters patent had failed of their purpose, and were ineffectual for good, and were productive of a harassing and mischievous uncertainty,—the Crown was advised by its own law officers to issue them no more, and the Church in the colonies betook itself, under the sanction of the same high legal authority that had exposed the worthlessness of the letters patent, to seek safety and order in the only way left open, on the basis of consensual contract, aided more or less by such legislation as might be had. I will give instances of what I mean.

(i.) Judgment *in re* the Bishop of Natal was delivered in March 1865. Within three or four months the Bishops of New Zealand petitioned the Queen to be allowed " to surrender their letters patent, and to be allowed to rely in future upon the powers inherent in their office for perpetuating the succession of their order within the Colony of New Zealand, and securing the due exercise of their episcopal functions, in conformity with the Church Constitution hereinafter described." This petition was based avowedly on the judgments of the Privy Council, Long *vs.* Bishop of Capetown, and *in re* the Bishop of Natal. The petitioners further " express their conviction that the right of appointment of bishops in New Zealand is not part of the prerogative of the Crown, inasmuch as all the bishoprics were founded by private efforts, and endowed from private resources." Finally, they " humbly pray that all doubts may be removed as to their status, both ecclesiastical and temporal ":—

1st. "By the acceptance of the surrender of their letters patent, now declared to be null and void.

2nd. "By declaring the Royal mandate under which your Majesty's petitioners were consecrated, to be merely an authority given by the Crown for the act of consecration, and to have no further effect or legal consequence.

3rd. " By recognising the inherent right of the Bishops of New Zealand to fill up vacancies in their own order by the consecration of persons elected in conformity with the regulations of the General Synod, without letters patent and without Royal mandate."

This petition was forwarded by the Secretary of State for the Colonies, Mr. Cardwell, to the Archbishop of Canterbury for his remarks. His Grace replied, " The substance of that petition seems to me to be the natural and necessary corollary from the two judgments of the Judicial Committee of the Privy Council referred to by the petitioners." I am unable to trace the rest of this correspondence, if there was any. I only know, what all know, that the Church in New Zealand has long been ordered exactly like our own, and that for its older designation—" The Church of England in New Zealand"— it has now substituted " The Church of the Ecclesiastical Province of New Zealand."*

(ii.) In the same year Lady (then Miss) Burdett Coutts, the munificent foundress of the Sees of Capetown, Adelaide in South Australia, and British Columbia and Vancouver's Island, addressed the Archbishop of Canterbury and Earl Russell, and the year following, the Queen, by petition, under cover of a very strong letter to Sir George Grey from the Bishop of London (Dr. Tait), complaining that the endowments provided by her for one object were in danger of being misapplied to another and different object, which she disapproved, involving the exemption of the colonial bishops, through defect of the letters patent, from the Crown's ancient jurisdiction over the state ecclesiastical, and praying that the defect might be remedied by legislation. Mr. Cardwell's reply to the Bishop of London states, among other things, " that in the opinion of Her Majesty's Government, it would be inconsistent with the settled principles of colonial policy to establish in the colonies by Imperial legislation a prerogative in respect to ecclesiastical matters which the highest court of appeal has declared to have no existence in

* Correspondence relative to Colonial Bishoprics. 1866, No. I. Blue-Book.

law. They have, however, caused a bill to be framed, and to be introduced into Parliament, which, without interfering in matters which fall within the sphere or local legislation, will, as they hope, have the effect of placing the Church of England at greater liberty to extend and perpetuate its ministrations throughout the colonial empire." (Correspondence relative to Colonial Bishoprics. Blue-Book, 1866.)

(iii). In consequence of the Judgment, *in re* the Bishop of Natal, it was determined that no more patents should be issued by the Crown for any bishops of Canada; and, accordingly, on the death of Bishop Mountain, no patent was issued for his successor in the see of Quebec, but simply a mandate for his conssecration, addressed to the Bishop of Montreal as Metropolitan. In 1866, however, on the election of the Archdeacon of Toronto (Bethune) to be coadjutor Bishop of Toronto under the title of Bishop of Niagara, it was determined that not even the mandate should be issued. Lord Carnarvon, as Secretary of State for the Colonies, thus writes to the Metropolitan Bishop of Montreal, under date, Downing-street, November 21st, 1866: " It appears by the recent decision of the Judicial Committee in the case of the Bishop of Natal, that Her Majesty has not the power to create a diocese, or assign a sphere of action to a bishop in a Colony in which an independent Legislature has been established. And it is the opinion of the law officers of the Crown, to whom I have caused this question to be submitted, that a mandate from the Crown is not necessary to enable colonial bishops to perform the act of consecration. It would not appear that the proposed mandate could have any legal effect; and, under such circumstances, it would hardly be consistent with the dignity of the Crown that Her Majesty should be advised to issue such mandate."*

---

* Colonial Church Chronicle, Feb., 1867, pp. 57—8.

(iv.) The Metropolitan Bishop of Sydney addressed Lord Kimberley in 1872 on the future appointments of colonial bishops, as well as on the *status* of priests and deacons of colonial ordination. Lord Blachford's Act (the Colonial Clergy Act) has since disposed of the second point. As to the first point, the Bishop of Sydney had asked " that Her Majesty may be advised to grant licence to the Archbishop of Canterbury to consecrate, and therein to name the diocese to which the bishop is to be consecrated ; . . . . and that such a course would be extremely expedient for reasons connected with property." The Under-Secretary replies " that Lord Kimberley is not prepared to recommend a departure from the course which has been adopted, after full consideration, under the advice of law-officers of the Crown. That course may be briefly summed up as follows :— Her Majesty will be advised to refuse, in conformity with the Judgment of the Judicial Committee, to appoint a bishop in any Colony possessing an independent Legislature, without the sanction of that Legislature ; but she will be advised, on the application of the Archbishop of Canterbury, to issue from time to time such mandate as is required by law to authorise the consecration of a bishop, no diocese or sphere of action, however, being assigned in such mandate.

" You are aware that colonial bishops may exercise, and, in fact, have exercised the power of consecration without Royal sanction ; and it remains for the colonial episcopate, having these facilities for containing their succession, to secure the position of their successors in respect to endowments or otherwise, by such voluntary agreement or local legislation as they may be advised is necessary or practicable."

---

* Colonial Church Chronicle, Sept., 1872, pp. 354—5.

(v.) Mauritius was constituted a Bishopric in 1854, Dr. Ryan being sent out as its first Bishop. In 1874, on the death of Bishop Huxtable, Her Majesty's Government determined not to issue any more letters patent. "As soon as this was made known to the Archbishop of Canterbury, arrangements were made for Bishop Ryan to come out to Mauritius to form a church body, which should hold in trust the church property of the diocese, and henceforth have the management of ecclesiastical affairs . . . . . A Synod was called together, consisting of eight Clergymen and nineteen Laymen. . . . . The opinion of the Synod was that steps should be immediately taken to have a Bishop sent out" . . . . "the choice" to be left "to the Archbishop of Canterbury."*

(vi.) On the demise of the late Bishop of Capetown, the fact was formally communicated through Governor Sir Henry Barkly to Lord Kimberley, Secretary of State for the Colonies. The reply from Lord Kimberley was as follows : "I have received with great regret the intelligence of the death of the Bishop of Capetown, conveyed in the Colonial Secretary's letter of the 19th ultimo." I may observe that I find no fault with this letter. On the contrary, I regard it as exactly befitting the occasion, on which there was nothing more to be done, and therefore nothing more to be said.

(vii.) In 1871 a Bill passed the Natal Legislature, which, had it become law, would have "vested the property granted for the use of the English Church, in the Bishop of Natal and his successors, thereby assuming that the Bishopric of Natal will be continued as an ecclesiastical corporation sole, by the appointment of future bishops in succession to the present Bishop."

* Colonial Church Chronicle, Sept., 1872 pp. 351—2.

The Queen, by an order in Council, referred this Bill to a Committee of Council, who recommended Her Majesty to withhold Her assent to the Bill. They state the grounds of their recommendation, in part, as follows:—" Their Lordships presume—having regard to the decisions of the Judicial Committee of your Majesty's Council, and the orders made thereon with reference to the letters patent granted by your Majesty to the Bishops of Capetown and Natal—that your Majesty will not be advised to appoint, by letters patent, any successors to the present Bishop of Natal; and they cannot advise your Majesty to assent to a Bill founded on an assumption that such an appointment will be made." [Report to Her Majesty the Queen of the Committee of Council on Bill No. 16 of 1871, passed by Legislative Council of Natal, &c., &c.]

Now what does this evidence prove? For every practical purpose, it proves conclusively two things: First, that the hypothesis that any day a patentee Bishop may drop down on Bishop Merriman, and forcibly and rightfully dispossess him of his throne, house, and income, may be safely dismissed. True; there is no Imperial Act forbidding such a re-issue of letters patent. But there are decisions of the Supreme Court of Appeal declaring that nothing short of an Act of the Imperial Legislature could give to letters patent so re-issued legal validity. And on those decisions not only have successive Secretaries of State, under the advice of successive law-officers of the Crown, reported through now many years in the terms above detailed, but Her Majesty has herself made orders which have identified Her executive authority with the judicial advice tendered to Her. There can be no receding from measures such as these. The other point established by all this evidence relates to the Judgment itself out of which the evidence has grown. To law has now been added usage; and the usage, originally based on the law, and interpretative of it under the highest official sanctions, has confirmed aud established the law.

Guided, then, by the light so obtained, how are we to estimate the letters patent of the first two Bishops of Grahamstown? They may have created what I think is sometimes called a lay-corporation, capable of taking an estate under a grant from the Crown. But having been granted after the Colony had received an independent Legislature, and not under the provisions of any statute, they could not create an ecclesiastical corporation, whose status, rights, and authority the Colony or any part of it could be required to recognise. They could not assign the Bishop any diocese, or give him any sphere of action. They could not give him jurisdiction over any person or persons, or give the Archbishop of Canterbury jurisdiction over him. And what the letters patent were ineffectual to do, must be counted as not done. A bishop so situated was the bishop only of a voluntary association. He could acquire authority as bishop only over those who contracted with him. He was in the same position, apparently, as the present Bishop of Capetown who was consecrated by Royal licence simply "to be a bishop, to the intent that he should exercise his functions in one of our possessions abroad." Suppose a bishop to have arrived on the spot nominally to be Bishop of Grahamstown, furnished with letters patent purporting to assign a diocese, and confer jurisdiction, but already known to be invalid, every equitable consideration and all right feeling might still have pointed to him as entitled to be received as bishop over the voluntary association over which he had come, under defective authorisation, to preside. But title he could have none, except on the footing of such contract as should subsequently be entered into.

Construed by the light since thrown on them by legal decisions of the very highest authority, and by now some years of constant usage in conformity with those decisions, it would seem impossible to read the letters patent of Bishops Armstrong and Cotterill in any other sense than the foregoing. In that case, Bishop Merriman's claim to be recognised as Bishop of Grahamstown would appear to differ from that of either of his predecessors, chiefly in that it rests on the basis of a sounder and broader contract, namely, a contract with the whole diocese at the time and in the act of his appointment and consecration. The English ecclesiastical system is diocesan and provincial. The *congé d' élire* testifies to the common-law right of every diocese, freely to elect its own bishop, as still in force.* Under the rules of our Provincial Synod of 1870, the work of the concurrent action of the entire province, the Diocese of Grahamstown, notably the Cathedral congregation, united to elect Bishop Merriman (then ex-Dean of Capetown) its bishop. "There is not a trace on the minutes," I am assured by one who has inspected them, " of anything like a protest, or an expression of dissent of any kind. The Secretaries reported to the President" (Dean Williams), "by whom it was communicated to the assembly, that the clerical members present, including those voting by proxy, had both individually and unanimously elected the Very Rev. N. J. Merriman, and that the lay members had both individually and unanimously assented to the same." The Bishops of the Province unanimously confirmed the election, and, with the exception of one who was unable to be present, took part in his consecration, in the same Cathedral in the chapter-house of which he had been chosen, in which he was after-

* See Appendix B.

wards enthroned, and from which by the decision of the Supreme Court he is now an outcast. What *legal* right did Bishops Armstrong and Cotterill enjoy more than Bishop Merriman that has the virtue of thus emptying Bishop Merriman's position of every other right that equitably, and *ex-contractu* belongs to it?

The only strictly legal right possessed by his predecessors under the letters patent more than Bishop Merriman enjoys without letters patent would appear to have been that affecting the trusteeship of S. George's Cathedral. The site on which the Cathedral is built first belonged to the Crown. In June, 1849, and November, 1850, grants of the land on which the Cathedral and certain neighbouring premises stand were made by the Crown to Bishop Gray. Under Act No 30 of 1860, which was framed partly for that purpose, Bishop Gray transferred the lands so vested in him to Bishop Cotterill. And in June, 1871, Bishop Cotterill made another transfer of the land in question (clearly not under Act 30 of 1860) to himself or the Bishop of Grahamstown for the time being, Archdeacon White or the Archdeacon of Grahamstown for the time being, the Registrar of the Diocese, and the Treasurer of the Board for the Endownment Fund of the See of Grahamstown. Of this last transfer, the Chief Justice says, " The defendant denies the validity of the transfer, on the ground that the requisite consent was not obtained ; but so long as the transfer, which is a judicial act, stands registered in the Deeds Office, it must be assumed to be valid until judicially set aside." I am no judge of the point of law, whether Bishop Merriman, being admitted to be Bishop of Grahamstown for the time being for every ecclesiastical purpose embraced within the contract between himself and the diocese in virtue of his election, consecration,

and enthronisation, could be held to be legally Bishop Cotterill's successor for the purposes of the trusteeship. How far the rule of *Cy-près* might be held by lawyers to apply to a case of this description, I can form no opinion. But this I know, that the Colonial Act No. 3 of 1873 was framed partly to meet the very case in hand, and that when Imperial legislation was contemplated that same year on purpose to provide for the transmission of property from bishops who were Royal patentees to " persons duly consecrated to the office of bishop, *having been accepted as successors of such bishops by the clergy and laity of the dioceses or reputed dioceses, concerned ;*" and when Lord Kimberley, then Secretary of State for the Colonies, consulted the various colonial churches—this among the number—by means of a circular letter, addressed to the various Colonial Governors, as to the need of such legislation, I was officially assured, being at the time Vicar-General, by Governor Sir Henry Barkly, in a letter dated Sept. 20, 1873, that, in the opinion of his responsible advisers, including the present Chief Justice, then Attorney-General, all such further legislation was for us unnecessary. His words are, " My responsible advisers are of opinion that there is no necessity, so far as this Colony is concerned, for Imperial legislation in regard to the future transmission of property vested in the Bishop or other office-bearers of the Church of England for ecclesiastical purposes,—the Colonial Act No. 3 of the present year having sufficiently provided for the regulation of all property held in trust for religious associations."*
My official reply to Sir Henry Barkly, for transmission to the Secretary of State, was largely influenced, as I need scarcely say, by the assurance which he had been authorised to give me; and, a considerable majority of colonies making similar replies, Lord Blachford's

* See Imperial Blue-Book, C.—979, 1874. Also the Appendix to this Pamphlet.

Act was passed the following year *minus* the property clauses.

If the silence of the recent Judgment, with reference to Act No. 2 of 1873, should turn out to mean that, in the Chief Justice's opinion, I was wrongly advised by the Colonial Government, the hardship of our case, already sufficiently heavy, will be proportionably the heavier. Meantime, Bishop Merriman, failing to answer the definition of a legal successor to Bishop Cotterill, as measured rigidly by the terms of the letters patent, is declared to be shut out from all estate in the Cathedral. As far as it has been necessary to adjudicate in this case, Bishop Merriman is pronounced not to be the Bishop of Grahamstown for the time being, and the See to be as good as vacant.

BISHOP MERRIMAN A SEPARATIST FROM THE CHURCH OF ENGLAND.

"But," the Chief Justice says, "a stronger and at the same time less technical objection to the plaintiff's title in respect of the Church of S. George still remains to be considered. That church was founded by and for the members of the Church of England." The land on which the church stands was granted by the Crown to Bishop Gray "upon the distinct trust that it should for ever thereafter be used for ecclesiastical purposes in connection with the Church of England, and for no other purpose or use whatever. But over and above the private trusts attaching to the church . . . the statute law of the land imposes upon those who have the custody of the church, and the administration of its affairs, the obligation to hold it in trust for the members of the Church of England in Grahamstown." The Judgment proceeds to cite, in support of these allegations, sundry provisions of the Graham's Town Church Ordinance, Act No. 2 of 1839, and Act 30 of 1860. Next is quoted a passage from the Judgment of the Privy Council (Long *vs.* Bishop of Cape Town) showing that for the purpose of the contract between Mr. Long and his Bishop, their Lordships took them "as having contracted that the laws of the Church of England shall, though only so far as applicable here, govern both." To this is added a quotation from the Master of the Rolls Judgment, to which the Chief Justice evidently attaches great importance, and which I therefore cite at length. " Where there is no State religion established by the Legislature in any Colony, and in such a Colony is found a number of persons who are members of the Church of England, and who establish a church there with the doctrines, rites, and ordinances of the Church of England, it is a part of the Church of England, and the members of it are, by implied agreement, bound by all its laws. In other words, the association is bound by the doctrines, rites, rules, and ordinances of the Church of England, except so far as any statutes may exist which (though relating to this subject) are confined in their operation to the limits of the United Kingdom of England and Ireland. Accordingly upon reference to the civil tribunal, in the event of any resistance to the order of the bishop in any such Colony, the court would have to inquire, not what were the peculiar opinions of the persons associated together in the Colony as members of the Church of England, but what were the discipline and doctrines of the Church of England itself, obedience to which doctrines and discipline the court would have to enforce."

The Chief Justice goes on: " We may take it, then, to be reasonably clear that under certain public statutes of this Colony, as well as under the title deeds affecting the property, the claims of all persons who assert any ecclesiastical rights in respect of S. George's Church, Grahamstown, must be decided according to the laws of the Church of England, so far as they are applicable here." This brings us to the crucial question, "By what religious body" was Bishop Merriman "appointed and consecrated as Bishop, and entrusted with the charge of the Diocese of Grahamstown? That religious body is admitted to be the Church of the Province of South Africa. If that body is a part or branch of the Church of England, and, as such, entitled to appoint bishops of dioceses of the Church of England in South Africa, this court would be bound to recognise its rights as against all members of the Church of England in the Diocese who interfere with them. If it is not a part or branch of the Church of England, it is difficult to see upon what grounds this court can be asked to impose its Bishop upon a congregation, consisting of members of the Church of England, in respect of a church which the public law of the land has devoted to ecclesiastical purposes in connection with the Church of England."

THE CHURCH OF ENGLAND *VS*. THE CHURCH OF THE PROVINCE OF SOUTH AFRICA.

The Chief Justice proceeds to dispose of the Church of the Province of South Africa, and of Bishop Merriman with it, by treating them as a separatist body; as much a separatist body, apparently, as if they had joined the Wesleyans or the Church of Rome. He identifies their point of departure from the Church of England with the Provincial Synod of 1870, and thus tacitly, but not indirectly, involves the whole Province in the schism. The actual history of the growth of the province, where it began, how it took shape, how the Cathedral congregation, represented not by the Dean alone but by its own formally elected lay-delegates, took part in the Synod of 1870, as well as in that of 1876, and helped to frame the very constitution and canons under which the same congregation subsequently conduced to Bishop Merriman's unanimous election;—all this the Judgment passes by, together with a great deal more, to which, however necessary to a full and fair estimate of the case, it was perhaps morally impossible, under all the circumstances, that the attention of the judges should have been particularly directed. The charge of separation, however, is grounded in a series of perfectly distinct considerations, which I will next proceed to examine.

i. First, absolute reliance seems to be placed on the name *Church of England*, as though it must mean one thing everywhere. "It is too late to contend, as has been done in the present case, that no legal identity can exist between the Church of England in South Africa and the Church of England in the mother country. That identity has been recognised by the two colonial statutes just mentioned (Act 2, 1839, and Act 30, 1860) and by the decisions of the Privy Council in the cases already quoted, and of the Master of the Rolls." Our offence would appear to present itself to the Chief Justice in the same light as if we had claimed to create a new Province under a new name in England itself, within the geographical limits of the Provinces of Canterbury or York, hold our own Synod independently of Convocation, frame our own laws in contempt of the Imperial Parliament, and set up our own tribunals, against those of the Sovereign, to apply our laws. I understand the argument against us to be that the name *Church of*

England is prohibitory of the name *Church of the Province of South Africa*, because the Church of England itself,—not the *name*, but the *thing named*,—is identically one and the same, here and at home.

The answer is that the name, Church of England, is a palpable equivoque, and determines nothing. If it did determine anything, it should be enough to cite the second of the " Preliminary Resolutions " prefixed to our constitution and canons : " That it is expedient that in all acts and documents the entire church, which comprehends the five aforesaid dioceses (Capetown, Grahamstown, Maritzburg, S. Helena, and the Orange Free State) should be called the Church of the Province of South Africa ; this title not being intended to exclude other titles (such as English or Anglican Church) under which this church, or any portion of it, may be known, but being used to express the fact that the whole church thus intituled is united in this provincial organisation, through which it is connected with other churches of the Anglican Communion and with the Church of England in particular." In the preamble to the constitution the alternative names are thus given, " otherwise known as the Church of England, or the English Church, or Church of the Anglican Communion in these parts." To which I may add that if any one will turn to Cardwell's Synodalia, he will find on a comparison of the Latin and English versions of the Laws Ecclesiastical, both being of authority, that " Church of England " is the invariable equivalent of " Ecclesia Anglicana." Why is the name, if so much weight is to be put upon the name " Church of England," to mean less in Bishop Merriman's mouth than in the Dean of Grahamstown's?

But the name, as a name, is a transparent equivoque. In England it means the geographical Provinces of Canterbury and York, with the dioceses which they respectively include, presided over by bishops who are peers of the realm. It means, besides such portion of the body of canon law as has obtained in England since the reformation on the footing of *consent, usage,* and *custom,* ——the entire collection of the statutes ecclesiastical, of which 263 are printed by Stephens as passed between the first year of George IV. and the eighth of Victoria ; not to speak of those passed before and since that period. It means the Houses of Convocation, the ecclesiastical Courts, together with the whole system of ecclesiastical judicature and administration, the Supremacy of the Crown in relation to the Established Church, grounded in old common-law rights and re-asserted by the statutes of Henry VIII. and Elizabeth, and whatever else appertains to the Church, as part of a system as old as England itself. Does any one suppose, or does the Chief Justice mean, that a private " Ordinance for authorising the appointment of a vestry and churchwardens for S. George's Church, Grahamstown" (Act. 2 of 1839), and an Act to " Enable the Bishops of Capetown and Grahamstown, respectively, to alienate, under certain conditions and restrictions, property vested in their respective sees" (Act. 30, 1860), can possibly have the incidental effect of extending the Church of England, in all its essential characteristics, into this country ? A Colonial Act for legalizing a select vestry, which is to possess powers and perform duties " according to the customs and usages of the United Church of England and Ireland," could no more extend to the Cape Colony the jurisdiction of the Court of Arches than it could abolish the House of Lords. Act 30 of 1860 mentions the Church of England in its interpretation clause once as follows : " In the interpretation of this Act the term " parish" shall mean any defined district of town or country placed by the bishop of the diocese, acting in accordance with the laws and usages of the Church of England *as received and accepted in this Colony* under the pastoral charge of a particular minister ; and the bishop and clergy mentioned in this Act shall mean the bishops and clergy of the said Church, &c., &c." The words above italicised plainly limit the terms "laws and usages" to what the Chief Justice himself admits when he says that all claims in respect of S. George's Church, Grahamstown, "must be decided according to the laws of the Church of England *so far as they are applicable here*," and are also a disclaimer of all those legal rights and obligations which are involved in the term Parish as known to the law of England. How can these two Acts be said to "recognise," and thus, I suppose, give a statutory confirmation to, the "*identity*" of the Church of England as by law established with the Church of England in the abridged and adapted condition—I speak of it now as a political not as a religious society—in which, if at all, it must exist here, on a purely voluntary basis? "To speak of inhabitants of a Colony, where there is no established church, as being members or forming part of the Established Church of England and Ireland, is nonsense, if we use that phrase in its literal acceptation as meaning the political society constituted under that name by law in England and Ireland. Where they (colonists) live, the laws that make that society do not exist, and the society itself, therefore, can have no existence. To use this expression therefore is to affirm, what some deny, that there is, under that name, a religious society as well as a political one ; and it really amounts to no more than an assertion that there are in the Colony persons accepting the same religious belief, the same forms of worship, and, so far as may be, the same or a like religious organisation as are accepted by the persons composing that religious society in England."* In keeping with this is the well-known saying of the late Bishop of Exeter, one of the best ecclesiastical lawyers that England ever produced, "that there is no Church of England out of England;" and also Lord Campbell's famous *dictum*† (Queen *vs.* Eton College) that "except in a few instances provided for by express statutes, as in the East Indies, a colonial bishop "has nothing in common with the English and Irish Bishops who belong to established churches, except that he is a Protestant bishop, canonically consecrated, and holding the faith of the Anglican Church." The Colonial Clergy Act, 1874,—the most recent Imperial legislation affecting the colonial church,— also distinguishes clearly, and in terms, between bishops of the Church of England and the orders conferred by them, on the one hand, and on the other, "bishops *not being bishops of the Church of England*," or a "bishop *other than a bishop of a diocese*" in England, viz., colonial bishops and their orders. (Compare Preamble with Sections 3 and 4). The Privy Council, too, distinctly admits the laws of the Church of England to be binding "only as far as applicable here," throws it upon us to determine how far they are applicable by framing our own rules for enforcing discipline, and further, declares it to be lawful for us to constitute our own tribunals for applying our rules.

As to our colonial church ordinances, nine in number, what has been already said of Act 2, 1839, substantially applies to them all. It may be added that, though not any one of them is in accordance with the common law of the Church of England,

---

* Remarks, &c., by Mountague Bernard, p 11.
† Queen's Bench Reports, Vol. VIII., Part III.

and all are more or less different from each other, they admit of a good defence and common sense explanation. The persons who sought a quasi-parochial incorporation under them were, individually, members of the English Church by law established. They sought the help of the local Legislature just for the reason that here there was no United Church of England and Ireland, and their object was fair and reasonable, when congregational self-government was all that was aimed at or thought of. The operation of these local ordinances has never been interfered with, and our provincial constitution, moreover, contains special provision for their due recognition, so long as they may continue unrepealed.

The battle of names is not worth further fighting. The Chief Justice himself admits the difference of designation not to be "decisive". According to English usage, to be a priest of the Province of Canterbury, or of the Province of York, is to be a priest of the Church of England. We say, on the same grounds, that to be a priest of the Province of South Africa is also to be a priest of the Church of England here, so far as the name Church of England is applicable to our circumstances. The dispute appeared childish, till the Supreme Court made questions of property, and of matters still more vital, to hinge on it. The Church of New Zealand, as has been already said, has lately exchanged the title of Church of England in New Zealand for the more exact official designation of the Church of the Ecclesiastical Province of New Zealand. Call ourselves what we may, we do not thereby alter our situation. If we would have bishops over us, all alike we must choose them, or depute others to choose them. All alike we must decide how far the laws of the Mother Church are applicable, if applicable at all ; must constitute our own tribunals, appoint our own judges, frame our own methods of pro cedure. We are all alike shut out from the English ecclesiastical courts. The English system, moreover, is essentially Diocesan and Provincial. As one Diocese cannot govern another, so one Province cannot govern another. The Sovereign, too, stands in a different legal relation to the Provinces of Canterbury and York from that in which She stands to our Province;—Her supremacy in relation to us here being identical with its relation to all other unestablished religious bodies, and the xxxviith Article, therefore, having the same significance for us all, as claiming for the Crown simply the same "Chief Government of all estates" against the Papal or any other foreign jurisdiction. No one name can adequately express our situation. But, the situation being what it is, if it unchurches Bishop Merriman, so far as the argument has at present proceeded, it equally unchurches Dean Williams.

SPECIFIC ACTS WHEREBY BISHOP MERRIMAN IS HELD TO HAVE CUT HIMSELF OFF FROM THE CHURCH OF ENGLAND.

But the Judgment, leaving the question of names, next proceeds to show that, beneath the difference of names, lie other differences of a more fundamental kind; to use the express words of the Judgment, instances of "more important departure from the laws of the Church of England." They are five in number.

(a.) The first article of our constitution stands as follows; and since comparatively few members of our Church know anything accurately of our synodical proceedings, I print it entire :—

"The Church of the Province of South Africa, otherwise known as the Church of England in these parts: First, receives and maintains the Faith of our Lord Jesus Christ as taught in the Holy Scriptures, held by the Primitive Church, summed up in the Creeds, and affirmed by the undisputed General Councils: Secondly, receives the Doctrine, Sacraments, and Discipline of Christ as the same are contained and commanded in Holy Scripture according as the Church of England has set forth the same in its Standards of Faith and Doctrine, and it receives the Book of Common Prayer, and of Ordering of Bishops, Priests, and Deacons, to be used, according to the form therein prescribed, in Public Prayer and Administration of the Sacraments and other Holy Offices; and it accepts the English version of the Holy Scriptures as appointed to be read in Churches; and, further, it disclaims for itself the right of altering any of the aforesaid Standards of Faith and Doctrine.

"Provided that nothing herein contained shall prevent the Church of this Province from accepting, if it shall so determine, any alterations in the Formularies of the Church (other than the Creeds) which may be adopted by the Church of England, or allowed by any General Synod, Council, Congress, or other Assembly of the Churches of the Anglican Communion; or from making at any time such adaptations and abridgments of, and additions to, the Services of the Church as may be required by the circumstances of this Province: Provided that all changes in, and additions to, the Services of the Church, made by the Church of this Province, shall be liable to revision by any General Synod of the Anglican Communion to which this Province shall be invited to send representatives.

"Provided, also, that in the intrepretation of the aforesaid Standards and Formularies the Church of this Province be not held to be bound by decisions, in questions of Faith and Doctrine or in questions of Discipline relating to Faith or Doctrine, other than those of its own Ecclesiastical Tribunals, or of such other Tribunal as may be accepted by the Provincial Synod as a Tribunal of Appeal."*

From the second of the foregoing provisos, the Chief Justice infers it to " be clear that the jurisdiction of the Queen in Council, in the interpretation of the " standards and formularies in questions of faith and doctrine," is not recognised by the Church of South Africa, and, as if to leave no doubt upon the matter, another canon (the 30th) emphatically declares that if any question should arise as to the interpretation of the canons or laws of this Church, or of any part thereof, the interpretation shall be governed by the general principles of canon law thereto applicable :"—a canon which the Chief Justice contrasts with certain well-known *dicta* of the Committee of Privy Council in the case of Williams *vs.* Bishop of Salisbury, as though, not content with having excluded the jurisdiction of the Sovereign, we had also imposed rules for the guidance of our tribunals in opposition to " the laws of England."

As to our 30th canon, it does no more than lay down the common sense principle, that inasmuch as our expressed rules, on the face of them, make no pretence to be a perfect code, they shall be interpreted, where they need interpretation, by the broad ascertained principles of the common law of the Church, as they have come down to us through post—reformation times, assured by custom, recognised by statutes, or in other ways. But what can be meant when we are said to have ignored the jurisdiction of the Queen in Council? The jurisdiction of the Queen's Courts is compulsory. Could we ignore the jurisdiction of

* Constitution and Canons of the Church of the Province of South Africa (Article 1., pp. 6, 7).

the Supreme Court of this Colony? The scenes recently enacted at Grahamstown are the answer. We are powerless against any decision of a Queen's Court. On the other hand, where the Queen has no legal jurisdiction, the mere agreement of private persons cannot set it up. The voluntary agreement, which is the basis of an arbitration, is wholly distinct from the authority which, under certain conditions, can alone give effect to an arbitration. Apparently, there is some confusion between the Judicial Committee, as it is empowered by statute to hear appeals in ecclesiastical suits from inferior ecclesiastical courts, which yet are Crown Courts, and the Queen in Council as the Court of Appeal from Her own civil tribunals here and elsewhere. "Nobody will seriously contend," says a high authority, several times quoted already, " that an appeal would lie from a sentence of deprivation by a Bishop of Natal, or any bishop similarly situated, to the Queen in Council, or will confuse with such a proceeding an appeal from a civil tribunal, like that prosecuted by Mr. Long. In the former case, there would be, in the eye of the law, no court, no cause, no judgment, and therefore no appeal: in the latter, the appeal is not from the Bishop's judgment, nor to the Crown as an ecclesiastical judge."* Solvitur ambulando. We *are* recognising the jurisdiction of the Sovereign, in the only way open to us, by appealing to the Privy Council against the Judgment of the Supreme Court, which also is a Court of the Sovereign. The Privy Council itself (Long *vs.* Bishop of Capetown) laid down for us the line we are pursuing. We can but go to such courts of the Sovereign as are open to us.

The proviso may lie open to the objection that it is superfluous. But its meaning is hardly doubtful.

---

* Remarks by Professor Mountague Bernard, p. 12.

It claims that any clergyman of this province, accused of heretical or false doctrine, shall stand on the same footing that he would occupy under like circumstances in England. The proof must depend on a comparison of the passages charged against him with "the true construction of those articles of religion and formularies referred to in each charge, according to the legal rules for the interpretation of statutes and written instruments."* In other words, the test of doctrinal truth here, as well as at home, must be the formularies, &c., which the accused has *subscribed*, not an unknown and ever-accumulating body of doctrinal decisions, bearing only indirectly on the particular case, which he could not possibly have subscribed, and which he may never have heard of. Such prosecutions have been declared to be of the nature of criminal proceedings. Our proviso accepts the ruling, and claims that, therefore, every such case, in the colonies as well as in England, stand on its own merits, as measured against the written law under which it comes. The proviso has no special reference to any Court of Final Appeal. If we choose to add to our Diocesan and Provincial Tribunals a Tribunal of Appeal in England, we must construct it for ourselves, as the Irish and Australian Churches have constructed theirs In any case it will stand on the same legal level with our lower Tribunals, in that its decisions will equally be no better than the decisions of arbitrators resting on the agreement of the parties, and dependent on the civil courts to give effect to them.

It has been said that one possible operation of the proviso might be to open the door in this Province to a clergyman deprived at home, suppose, for inculcating the worship of the B. Virgin. But to

---

* Williams *vs*. Bishop of Salisbury.

this, our Canon 12, Section II., is a complete answer: forbidding, as it does, any bishop of this province to institute any clergyman to a pastoral charge in his diocese, until such clergyman have produced, besides his letters of orders, the testimonials required for institution, subscribed by three or more priests, and countersigned by the bishop of the diocese where he last served, and until he shall have satisfied the bishop into whose diocese he seeks admission, of his " learning, *soundness in the faith*, and innocency of life and conversation."

It also deserves notice, that the limitation involved in the proviso would appear to denote that in questions *other than* questions of faith and doctrine, or of discipline relating thereto, we accept the custom and ruling of the Mother Church as binding.

(b.) But Article I. of our Constitution contains another " separatist " proviso. Having tied ourselves, hand and foot, to the doctrines and formularies of the Church of England;—having disclaimed the right of altering any of the aforesaid standards of faith and doctrine;—we provide that we are not thereby to be understood to have precluded ourselves " from *accepting* any alterations in the formularies of the Church (*other than the Creeds*) which may be adopted by the Church of England, or allowed by any General Synod, Council, Congress, or other Assembly of the Churches of the Anglican Communion ";—it being further provided that any alterations in or additions to the services of the Church made by this Province shall be liable to revision by superior authority. We are supposed to have " seriously departed from the doctrines of the Church of England " by having reserved to ourselves, as a Province, the right by implication *not* to accept whatever alterations may hereafter be made in the Prayer Book at home, and particularly by a parenthetical mention of the Creeds as, in our judgment, unalterable. In 1872, when the Convocation of Canterbury had agreed to append to the Athanasian Creed a certain Synodical Declaration "for the removal of doubts, and to prevent disquietude in the use of the Creed," the Convocation of York proved its independence by rejecting the recommendation. To deny our Provincial Synod the same independence would be contrary to the system of the Church of England. We further assume, and we are not ashamed of the assumption, that we hold the Creeds to be of higher authority than the decree of any Synod, provincial or national. Whatever the civil courts of this Colony may determine, the time is not come yet when the Church of England, by altering the Catholic Faith, will constitute us separatists for adhering to it. How, on such grounds, we can be separatists, liable to the confiscation of our Church property, *in prospectu*, it is still more difficult to conceive. It is as if a beneficed clergyman in England were summarily deprived for announcing that in the event of the Imperial Parliament at some future time proscribing the use of the Apostles' Creed he should refuse obedience to such a law.

(c.) The third instance of our disloyalty to the Church of England is found in Canon 3—*Of election of Bishops*. "In none" (of our rules) "is any licence, mandate, or consent of the Crown, or its representative in the Colony, required; in none of them is the Crown or its representative even mentioned." This point has been sufficiently discussed already; nor is it worth while to go into the question as to whether, or how far, we were entitled to consider the letters patent a hindrance rather than an aid to the development of the Colonial Church. The Synod of 1870 was "of opinion that the resignation" by the Bishops of Capetown and Grahamstown "of their Sees, as held under letters patent, would for the present be inexpedient." In so deciding, the Synod took the course, as I think, most respectful to the Crown, and, in every sense, the most moderate. To say that "in none of our rules" (affecting the appointment of our bishops) "is the Crown mentioned," is a mistake. The second proviso of Article XV. of our Constitution in terms excepts from the ordinary operation of those rules "any diocese in which a successor to the vacant see shall be appointed by the Crown under letters patent giving legal jurisdiction." The VIIth of our Preliminary Resolutions asserts the same principle, with a particular application to the Diocese of S. Helena. Acting in a like spirit, when in 1864 the Duke of Newcastle, then Secretary of State for the Colonies, obtained for us the direction of the law-officers of the Crown touching certain acts of previous Synods, whereby some imputation of illegality had been incurred, we complied with the advice tendered in every particular (See Constitutions, Acts, &c., of the third Synod of the Diocese of Capetown, 1865), and a copy of our Rules, as amended, was at once forwarded to the Secretary of State through the Governor. To have treated the Royal Mandate, 1870, as necessary for the valid consecration of our bishops, would have been to close our memories to the history of the Colonial Church during the preceding seven years.

(d.) But, the Judgment proceeds, "Neither the Synod of 1870, nor that of 1876, was attended by the Bishop of Natal. . . . . . That he was expressly excluded is clear. . . . . . By what process of reasoning can a Church which excludes from its communion and from its Provincial Synods a Bishop of the Church of England, having a Diocese within the Province, claim to be part and parcel of the Church of England?" I will explain.

After private, brotherly, and tender efforts made in vain to win Bishop Colenso to reconsider his books and his responsibilities, in February, 1863, twenty-five

English Bishops, ten Irish, four Colonial, and two ex-colonial Bishops, united in calling upon him, in terms studiously gentle, but more formally, to weigh the solemn question whether, should he adhere to his published avowals and opinions, he could honestly retain his position. This letter was signed, among others, by both the English and both the Irish Archbishops, and the then Bishop of London, Dr. Tait. On the following 23rd of March, the Archbishop of Canterbury issued this circular to all the Bishops:—
"I herewith forward to you a copy of the resolution to which you gave your assent at the meeting in the beginning of February. I wish to inform you that I am myself about to act on it." (Signed) C. T. Cantuar. The resolution stood as follows:—"That, having regard to the grievous scandal to the Church occasioned by certain books published under the name of the Bishop of Natal, and not disavowed by him, we, the undersigned, express our own resolution not to allow the said Bishop to minister in the Word or Sacraments within our several dioceses until the said Bishop shall have cleared himself from such scandal."*

Having been eventually deposed from his office by the Court of his own Province, the Privy Council pronounced the proceedings null and void in law. Lord Romilly, consistently with the previous decision, gave him back his income, and a later decision of the Privy Council confirmed his legal estate in the Church property of the Diocese of Natal. The sentence of deposition, however, as a spiritual act, was, in one form or other, accepted by the Convocations of Canterbury and York; by the General Convention of the Church of the United States; by the Bishops of the Scottish Episcopal Church; by the Provincial Synod of the Church in Canada; and by fifty-six Bishops of the Lambeth Conference in 1867. During one of his

---

* Life of Robert Gray. Vol. II., pp. 18—55.

visits to England, Bishop Colenso was advertised as intending to preach in a church within the Diocese of Peterborough. The then Bishop (Dr. Jeune) at once inhibited him. On the occasion of another and later visit, he attempted to preach at Oxford. The Bishop (Dr. Mackarness) at once inhibited him. The Bishop of London (Dr. Jackson) about the same time issued a general inhibition forbidding him to minister within the Diocese of London. He subsequently preached in the chapel of Balliol College, which is to all intents as a private room, and was offered the pulpit of Westminister Abbey by Dean Stanley, but declined the invitation. To the last Lambeth Conference, attended by a hundred bishops, he was not invited. By our exclusion of Bishop Colenso from our provincial councils and fellowship, we are declared by the Supreme Court to have "separated" ourselves "root and branch from the Church of England." Did the Bishops who agreed in February 1863 to inhibit Bishop Colenso in the event of his declining to retract, and the Bishops of London, Oxford, and Peterborough, who subsequently, when occasion for doing so arose, put the resolution in force, thereby inflict upon themselves the same sentence of excision? Did they become "root and branch" separatists from the Church of England, equally with us? And how stands the Archbishop of Canterbury himself, from whom the invitations to the Lambeth Conference proceeded?

Bishop Colenso's restoration to the Church,—his *legal* position I, of course, do not challenge,—would be matter of rejoicing to me, and to thousands more. No one who knows anything of his career can seriously suppose that he does not deny the Faith, as our Prayer Book embodies it, in fundamentals, or can help seeing that Stopford Brooke has shown him what ought to have been his course long since.

Whether of the two, our Provincial Synod, in excluding Bishop Colenso, or Dean Williams, in making common cause with him as he has done,—has the better right to be said to represent the Church of England in its present relations to Bishop Colenso, let the action of the English Bishops declare. The Judgment certainly goes great lengths when it makes the inclusion or exclusion of Bishop Colenso in connection with the meeting of voluntary religious bodies a test of Communion, virtually pronouncing those not in Communion with Colenso to be out of Communion with the Church of England.

(e.) The fifth and last indictment against our rules is that Canons 24 and 25 (of Vestries and of Churchwardens and Sidesmen) " appear to infringe upon the special laws made by the Colonial Legislature for the management of S. George's Church." But this again is a mistake. Article XVI. of our Constitution provides expressly for the case of Grahamstown, and all similar cases, covering both questions of property, and matters generally of parochial concern. It stands as follows :—" The Provincial Synod shall frame such regulations as may be necessary from time to time for the management of property held in trust for the Church of this Province—save and except the properties in the Dioceses of Capetown and Grahamstown heretofore acquired—and shall have full power and authority, except so far as the same shall be ordered by law, or prescribed by the terms of any special trust, to determine in what manner, and upon what conditions, such property shall be used or occupied. It shall also have power, except such matters be otherwise ordered by law or by terms of any special trust, to determine how and by whom patronage shall be exercised, and what shall be the duties of parochial officers and the rights and privileges of parishioners in Church matters, and further, to frame rules as regards the division and boundaries of parishes, and other such questions."

The concluding words of this part of the Judgment demand a moment's separate consideration. "In and over the religious body," says the Chief Justice, "which has appointed the plaintiff as its chief pastor, he is a Bishop entitled to exercise the spiritual functions and consensual authority of a Bishop, and within any church lawfully devoted to the ecclesiastical uses of that body he is entitled to perform all those episcopal functions which appertain to his office according to the rules and canons of that body; but he has not, as of right, any episcopal authority in and over the Church of England as received and accepted in this Colony, or within any church devoted by law or by private deeds of trust to the uses of the Church of England."

Now the Church of England, *as received and accepted in this Colony*, in any fair and intelligible sense of those words, is identical with the Church of the Province of South Africa. There is no intelligible sense in which the Church of England here can be said to be *identical* with the Church by law established at home. But if these positions be disputed, there is at least no question as to what religious body appointed the plaintiff its chief pastor. That body was the Diocese of Grahamstown, signally the Cathedral congregation. That parish, being duly represented both at the Synod of 1870, and in the elective Assembly in 1871, was second to none in heartiness and zeal on either occasion. The Cathedral was the place where the electors met; in the Cathedral they invoked God's presence and blessing on what they were about to do; the election took place in the Cathedral chapter-house; the minutes of the election were entered on the Cathedral records; in the Cathedral Bishop Merriman was consecrated, there he was enthroned, and with that building he never ceased to be identified as the lawful Bishop of Grahamstown, until the other day, when, by one of those surprises in which law is fertile, it was successfully pleaded that the Cathedral, with its Dean and congregation, belonged to one religious community, and Bishop Merriman to another.

II. WHAT ARE THE RIGHTS OF THE DEFENDANT IN RESPECT OF THE *CATHEDRAL CHURCH*, AS RECTOR AND DEAN?

After what has been already said, the case for the defendant admits of being brought within comparatively narrow bounds. It is admitted that Dean Williams was appointed Colonial Chaplain by the Government, on Bishop Cotterill's nomination, in 1865, and that he was subsequently authorised to assume the titles of Rector and Dean, but whether under any formal instrument, or by any regular process of any kind, is uncertain. It is also admitted that on October 20th of the same year, Dean Williams took and subscribed the oath of canonical obedience to the Bishop of Grahamstown and his successors, and, further, made declaration of his submission " to the rules and regulations of the Synod of the Diocese of Grahamstown in all things which shall not be contrary to the laws of the United Church of England and Ireland." Having regard to all the facts, the Chief Justice concludes that were Bishop Merriman such a Bishop as Bishop Cotterill was, then the defendant would have been equally bound to him, on the footing of the contract " that the laws of the Church of England should, as far as applicable here, govern both." (Long *vs.* Bishop of Capetown).

The contention for the Dean is that the relations between him and Bishop Cotterill began on an honest Church of England basis, and that the rules and regulations of the Diocesan Synods of 1860 and 1863 —the only synodical rules in existence in the diocese when the Dean made his subscription,—also rested on an honest Church of England basis. But at some subsequent time, so runs the story, a division arose within the diocese. Certain parties agreed to " found a Church distinct from the Church of England." They did " found " such a Church, repudiating the rightful headship of the Sovereign, ignoring letters patent, and making laws contrarient to those of the Church of England, as well as to certain colonial statutes binding on all true members of that Church. Bishop Merriman is the creation of this new and distinct religious body, and as such can have neither part nor lot in the older community which Bishop Cotterill represented, and to which Dean Williams belongs still. Such, in sum and substance, is the history of the rise of the Church of the Province of South Africa, and of the Dean's relations to it, as recognised or assumed throughout the argument of the Chief Justice. My reply is that this is pure theory, contradicted by the facts.

In limine, if such a new and distinct Church, as has been said, was ever founded, Bishop Cotterill and the Dean were foremost among its founders. The Dean did not *join* it; he united with his Bishop on the one hand, and with his congregation on the other, to *found* it;-- that is to say, so far as the Diocese of Grahamstown was concerned in the movement. The true history of events may be more accurately stated thus: The creation of the See of Grahamstown was part of a wider scheme creating or purporting to create a Metropolitan

See or Province. The letters patent issued to the Metropolitan Bishop, as well as to his suffragans, under this arrangement, were necessarily all of equal validity, or invalidity, as we may choose to express it. By degrees it became apparent that the days of letters patent, under conditions such as ours, were past and gone for ever. The Imperial Government, again and again appealed to, again and again pointed to the decision of the Privy Council in the matter of the Bishop of Natal as final. Letters patent may have created a corporation capable of taking grants of land. Otherwise, they were void in law, and would be issued no more. Meantime, in South Africa, as in Canada and elsewhere, the Colonial Church, urged by its inherent vitality, refused to stand still, or to die out. By slow and cautious stages, our several Dioceses began to close in, and take the common action incumbent on a Province, along the lines broadly marked out for them by the joint action of the civil and ecclesiastical authorities. It was this action that the Chief Justice,—unavoidably—he will pardon me for saying—a stranger to our system,—has evidently mistaken for the founding of a new Church. Diocesan action preceded Provincial action. Necessarily so ; for Provincial action means the convergence to one point of sundry separate lines of Diocesan action. Further, Provincial action is essentially legislative. It is the action to which we mainly look to give oneness to our Diocesan system, although the Provincial Synod itself is but one of a graduated series. And thus when at last our Bishops,—Bishop Cotterill, as I have said, among the foremost of them,—judged the time to have come for summoning our first Provincial Synod, all loyal and intelligent churchmen hailed it as a new point of departure indeed, but only as men rejoice when they have crowned the arch with the keystone. The Provincial Synods of 1870 and

1876 may lie open to objection, or they may not; but it is certain that they stand in a direct, necessary, organic connection with the Diocesan Synods of 1860 and 1863, which Dean Williams subscribed, and his subscription to which—as the Chief Justice admits,—may be assumed to have been a condition of his obtaining the dignity of Dean. Let us look at the documentary evidence of this assertion.

Chapter I. of the Acts, &c., &c., of the Synod of Grahamstown (first and second Sessions, 1863), lays down the constitution of the Synod to consist of Bishop, clergy, and laity under certain self-imposed rules and conditions. Chapter VII. provides "a Diocesan Tribunal for the exercise of ecclesiastical discipline." This, clearly, was the act of a voluntary body. The Synod was held without licence of the Crown; nor was the assent of the Sovereign asked to what it did. What powers greater than these were assumed by the Synod of 1870? The Synod also lays down rules regulating the exercise of patronage. It prescribes "instructions for the guidance and information of ministers and parishioners, in the Diocese of Grahamstown, relative to the choice and duties of churchwardens and sidesmen, the summoning and conduct of vestry meetings, and other necessary parochial matters, in cases wherein these matters are not already provided for by local ordinance." It defines a parishioner to be "every male member of the Church, being of the full age of eighteen years." And it passes a resolution that "four clerical and four lay members be elected by ballot, by clergy and laity respectively, in such manner as the Bishop may determine, to sit in a Provincial Synod, should one be summoned before the next meeting of the Synod of the Diocese."

To the Acts, &c., &c., *of the Synod of* 1867 (*third Session*) is prefixed a declaration:—" 1. That the Synod, on behalf of the Diocese, accepts the position *in which it* (the Diocese) *has hitherto stood*, as one of *the Dioceses of the Province of South Africa*, &c., &c. 2. That, in the opinion of this Synod, it is desirable that a Provincial Synod should be held at an early period, in order to agree upon those matters which are necessary for the Church Government of this Province, &c., &c. 3. That . . . . this Diocese should be represented in the Provincial Synod . . . not only by its Bishop, but by representatives of its clergy and laity, &c., &c. 4. That . . . a Provincial Synod should provide a Tribunal of Appeal from any sentences pronounced by a Diocesan Tribunal, &c. &c. 5. That this Synod, recognising the need of some Court of Final Appeal in ecclesiastical causes, ... requests the Lord Bishop of Grahamstown to bring the subject before the Congress of English and Colonial Bishops about to assemble at Lambeth, &c., &c. 6. That the consideration of the constitution of any Final Court of Appeal for this Diocese be postponed till after the approaching meeting of the Bishops of the whole English Church at Lambeth. 7. That this Synod considers it necessary, without delay, to make provision for the mode of appointment of Bishops to the See of Grahamstown as vacancies may occur. 8. That . . . . the voice of the Church in the Diocese, expressed through its clerical and lay representatives assembled in Synod should be heard before any appointment to the vacant See shall be completed. 9. That the Dean and Chapter be empowered, in the event of emergency . . . . to summon the Synod of the Diocese. 10. That this Synod . . . . sitting now for the first time after the meeting of the Provincial Synod of Bishops in December, 1863, feels it a duty not to separate without humbly expressing its dutiful acceptance of the condemnation pronounced on the teaching contained in the writings of the Right Reverend Dr. Colenso, subject to any review of the sentence before a higher tribunal." Chapter xiii. includes the following resolutions relating to a capitular body: "That . . . it is necessary, in order to carry out the Cathedral system and the action of a capitular body in the Cathedral Church of S. George, that the Ordinance affecting that Church should be repealed, and this Synod hopes that action with that object may be taken by the parishioners of S. George's in accordance with the petitions from the Synod of 1860 to both Houses of Parliament, which were drawn up and signed by the representatives of the said Cathedral Church in the Synod then held." And "That the Lord Bishop be respectfully requested to draw up in consultation with the Dean and Chapter . . . . a code of statutes for the said capitular body." The ratification of the acts, &c., &c., of this Synod, dated July 1, 1867, stands signed by the Bishop (Bishop Cotterill), F. H. Williams, Dean and Rector of S. George's Cathedral, and the Clerical Secretary.

"The first Lambeth Conference met in September and December of the same year (1867), and the inter-relations of the Home and Colonial Churches formed the most prominent subject of discussion. The importance of the Resolutions adopted at that Conference, in their bearings on the history of the Church of this Province, cannot be estimated duly without particular and careful examination of the subject. It is not too much to say that, coupled with the Reports of the Committees appointed under the Conference, those Resolutions present the basis on which our whole Provincial action was grounded. Take for instance, Resolution VIII:—"That, in order to the binding of the Churches of our Colonial Em-

pire, and the Missionary Churches beyond them, in the closest union with the Mother Church, it is necessary that they receive and maintain without alteration the standards of faith and doctrine as now in use in that Church."—(I beg to call attention to the qualifying words " *now in use.*").—" That, nevertheless, each Province should have the right to make such adaptations and additions to the services of the Church as its peculiar circumstances may require : *Provided*, that no change or addition be made inconsistent with the spirit and principles of the Book of Common Prayer, and that all such changes be liable to revision by any Synod of the Anglican Communion in which the said Province shall be represented."*
In 1869 the Synod of the Diocese of Grahamstown (fourth Session) formally accepted the foregoing Resolution ; as it also did the principles laid down in the Lambeth Report I., as regards the relations and functions of Diocesan and Provincial Synods ; and those enunciated in Report IV. with reference to the election of Bishops. It further resolved, " That the Synod of this Diocese in the Session of 1867, having referred certain questions of great moment to the Assembly of Bishops at Lambeth, this Synod (1869) thankfully acknowledges the assistance given to it by the reports of the committees of that Assembly, laid on the table by the Bishop." Dean Williams, it is needless to say, was an active and prominent member of all these Synods. The next year (1870) the first full Provincial Synod met at Capetown, and the Province was organised.

Now, is this a true account of the order of events, or is it not? If it is, where is the point between 1863 and 1870 on which any man alive may put his finger, and say, " *Here* the members of the Church of England

---

* Conference of Bishops of the Anglican Communion holden at Lambeth, &c., 1867, p. 17.

in South Africa, having been faithful once, made a new—a schismatical—departure, and "founded a distinct Church?" It is quite true that between 1863 and 1870, mainly in consequence of the decision of the Privy Council in the matter of the Bishop of Natal, a change of view passed over the whole Colonial Church, which influenced its action. The term "Church of England" ceased to mean for the Colonies what we all at one time believed it to mean. But it is not true that Dean Williams attached himself to a new and distinct religious body when he joined the Provincial Synod of 1870. He went to that Synod a member of the very same religious body by which he contracted to be ruled when he took the oath of canonical obedience, and submitted himself to the Diocesan Synod of Grahamstown "in all things which shall not be contrary to the laws of the United Church of England and Ireland;" *i.e.*, as again and again acknowledged, *so far as those laws are applicable here*. Nor can the opposite to this be maintained by any reasoning which will not tend to neutralise the whole principle of consensual contract, and to shake every religious organisation founded on such contracts to their base.

III. HAS THE DEFENDANT, BY HIS ACTS AND CONDUCT SUBSEQUENT TO HIS APPOINTMENT, CONFERRED UPON THE PLAINTIFF THE RIGHT WHICH HE SEEKS TO ESTABLISH BY THIS ACTION?

The question, if I understand it, is this :—Admitting what the Chief Justice declares it "idle" to deny, that Dean Williams, by the part which he took in the Provincial Synod of 1870, became personally subject to its rules and canons, and that he personally subjected himself to Bishop Merriman's episcopal jurisdiction by the part he took in his election ;—is the Dean thereby estopped from denying the Bishop's rights, on the ground of his not being a lawful Bishop of the Church of England? The hypothesis is that Dean Williams began in 1865 by being a Rector and Dean of the Church of England in Grahamstown ; that in 1870, without any change or disturbance of titles, office, residence, duties, emoluments, or relation to his flock, or even to his vestry and churchwardens under the Grahamstown Church Ordinance, the Dean took an active part in founding a separatist and illegal association, cutting himself off thereby, " root and branch," from the Church of England ; that in 1871 he further took a prominent part in constituting Bishop Merriman Bishop of the new and separatist association ; that for over eight years, notwithstanding disagreements, he continued to recognise Bishop Merriman under the association as his lawful Bishop ; but that, eventually, having incurred the exercise of discipline under the rules of the new community, he disowned it, and on the strength of his mere unsupported word that he did so, returned to the Church of England again, leaving Bishop Merriman behind him. On this hypothesis, I confess I do not see why the Dean should be held to be estopped from doing whatever he likes. I have already anticipated what I believe to be the true answer, by what has been said in the course of other portions of the argument. The maxim " *Pacta, quæ contra leges constitutionesque fiunt nullam vim habere, indubitati juris est,*" has, I submit, no bearing on the case. The hypothesis melts away before a full and steady regard to the facts.

IV. ARE THE RESPECTIVE RIGHTS OF THE PARTIES IN ANY WAY AFFECTED BY THE DECISIONS OF THE DIOCESAN COURTS?

This inquiry is met by the same considerations that were urged in answer to that immediately preceding it. The hypothesis assumes Dean Williams, being still rightfully and securely possessed of a certain position and income obtained by him as a clergyman of the Church of England, to have become justly amenable to the jurisdiction of a certain ecclesiastical Tribunal representing a distinct and separatist religious body, by union with which he cut himself off "root and branch" from the Church of England. It is as if Cardinal Newman had openly joined the Church of Rome, still continuing to be openly Vicar of S. Mary's, Oxford, and in the uninterrupted and unquestioned enjoyment of any other emoluments previously acquired by him in the Church of England. The hypothesis must be that he subsequently renders himself liable to discipline in the Church of Rome, and under that system is suspended, with loss of income, and is otherwise sentenced. But the Church of Rome has bestowed on him no office! It cannot take away what it never gave; nor can it touch the position of the Vicar of S. Mary's, which has to do with an altogether different community. The hypothesis involves so many contradictions and impossibilities that no arrangement of language can give consistency to it. My answer is that, as it appears to me, it is at variance with the facts, and that the Diocesan Tribunal which sentenced Dean Williams did truly represent the authority of identically the same religious body, whatever may be its correct designation, to which Bishop Cotterill originally appointed him.

LEGISLATION RECOMMENDED AS THE EFFECTUAL REMEDY FOR OUR TROUBLES.

I pass by some other minor objections to the plaintiff's claims, raised by the Chief Justice, which were not argued, and proceed to consider briefly the advice of the Court that we, in any case, betake ourselves to the Legislature, Imperial or Colonial, for our only true and permanent remedy. "If the Privy Council," the Chief Justice says, " should see its way clear to decide in the plaintiff's favour, I, for my part, shall not regret the result. But whatever course may be taken in respect of this action, I feel bound to express my individual opinion as to the necessity of legislation, whether Imperial or Colonial, to regulate the relative rights of the Church of South Africa and the Church of England, in respect to their endowments under private deeds of trust, and to legalise the transfer to the Church of the Province of South Africa of property secured by the law for the uses of the Church of England, in those cases in which there has been acquiescence for a certain length of time, or where a majority of the congregation consent to the transfer." And Mr. Justice Smith says, "I have a firm conviction that nothing short of an Act of Parliament can finally and satisfactorily settle the whole question of property. I strongly advise the Church of South Africa to modify their constitution and canons, and to apply to Parliament."

For my own part, I adhere to the opinion which I expressed officially to Governor Sir Henry Barkly for transmission to the Secretary of State, supported by the present Chief Justice when he was Attorney-General, in October, 1873, that in Act 3 of 1873, we have all the legislation that we require. It must be borne in mind, however, that that Act is applicable to us only as an Episcopal, not as a Presbyterian or Congregationalist body. Episcopacy means not so many groups of independent congregations, each group or congregation taking for its Bishop whom it will, or can procure, but a number of territorial divisions called Dioceses, each under its own Bishop, or a number of Provinces, each including a number of Dioceses, and under its own Metropolitan, through whom alone all the parts and members of any one Diocese or Province have visible communion with the rest of the Church. On this foundation the Lambeth Conference of 1878 took its stand, laying down, as primary principles of Church order necessary for the maintainance of union among the Churches of our Communion :—(1.) "That the duly certified action of every national or particular Church, and of each ecclesiastical Province (or Diocese not included in a Province), in the exercise of its own discipline, should be respected by all the other Churches, and by their individual members. (2.) That when a Diocese, or territorial sphere of administration, has been constituted by the authority of any Church or Province of this communion within its own limits, no Bishop or other clergyman of any other Church should exercise his functions within that Diocese without the consent of the Bishop thereof. (3.) That no Bishop should authorise to officiate in his Diocese a clergyman coming from another Church or Province, unless such clergyman present letters testimonial, countersigned by the Bishop of the Diocese from which he comes."* Among the Churches claiming to be thus united are " the Church of England, and the Churches planted by her in India, and the Colonies," including the Province of South Africa. Now, the principles involved in these terms of union and intercommunion are fundamental to the idea of

---

* Conference of Bishops, &c., &c , holden at Lambeth, July, 1878, pp. 12 and 13.

Episcopacy. In them the strength of Episcopacy lies. No property arrangements can be accepted except such as are subordinate to them. If our property, all or any of it, is to be wrested from us on the grounds advanced by the recent Judgment, be it so. We can never consent to divide our spiritual heritage of order and mission, derived to us from Christ through the Church of England, with a nominal Church of Englandism founded in a repudiation of the only Episcopacy which the Church of England can supply to it, or recognise.

CONCLUDING REMARKS.

To what has been said, chiefly in answer to arguments not deemed conclusive, much more might be added in the way of positive proof of the loyal spirit in which our Provincial organisation has been built up. Every instance in which we are supposed to have exceeded our due liberty as a voluntary body has been carefully noted against us. It is remarkable that no regard seems to have been paid to the evidence afforded by our declaration of Fundamental Principles and the Articles of our Constitution, as well as by our Rules and Resolutions, of our hearty and fixed resolve to abide in the closest spiritual and doctrinal union and visible communion with our dear Mother Church of England that with God's blessing and in the nature of the case is possible. We have more than anticipated, by the terms of our incorporation as a Province, all that the late Lambeth Conference, comprising a hundred Bishops, in 1878, declared to be in that regard necessary.* So far as the Judg-

---

* Report of Committee on the best mode of maintaining union among the various Churches of the Anglican Communion. Conference of Bishops, July, 1878, p. 10, &c.

ments of the Privy Council, or the instructions of the Government, based on the opinions of the law-officers of the Crown,* have marked out our course for us, we have scrupulously followed it The Rolls Judgment decided the single point that the annual income of the fund appropriated for the endowment of the Bishopric of Natal should be paid to Bishop Colenso. But, as Professor Bernard says, "No court can decide a question not brought before it; nor can language the most laboriously positive transform a *dictum* into anything more than an expression of opinion."† Lord Romilly's conclusion followed by necessary sequence that of the Privy Council. The trains of reasoning by which those two conclusions were respectively obtained have been pronounced by no less distinguished a lawyer than Professor Bernard to be in some principal particulars irreconcileable. Successive Governments, apparently without hesitation, have adopted the decision of the Privy Council in the matter of the Bishop of Natal, together with the reasoning that led up to it. The Colonial Church has had no option but to do the same. The task laid on us has been to determine how far the laws of the Church of England are applicable to our situation. We claim to have done our best to fulfil this task dutifully and honestly. We have not interpreted our duty as the Supreme Court has interpreted it for us. But it has not been shown that we have broken any law; it might have been shown that there is an Imperial Act (the Colonial Clergy Act, 1874), which is from first to last a running recognition of the status of the Colonial Church, as this and other Colonies now exemplify it. That Act would appear to be a point-blank

---

* Correspondence between Duke of Newcastle and Bishop of Capetown, 1863-4.
† Remarks, &c., p. 5.

confutation of the Colonial Church of Englandism which the late Judgment upholds. The conditional status which it assigns to Colonially-ordained Clergymen—Clergymen ordained Deacon or Priest by Bishops such as Bishop Merriman,—at once defines what such Clergymen *are not*, compared with Clergymen ordained by the Bishop of a Diocese in England, and what such Clergymen *are*, compared with what their position would be were they separatists. It were needless to say that the status thus assured to this Church by the Imperial Legislature is accepted, as of course, by the whole English Episcopate. Can a Colonial Law-Court over-ride an Imperial Act? I should be surprised to hear that it could. Add to this, that there are ties, binding communities together, that are stronger than human laws. We are bound, as we believe, to our dear Mother Church of England by links which Parliaments could never have created, and which no law-courts can dissolve. When at the Wolverhampton Congress in 1867, in the course of a speech by Bishop Selwyn, one who was present interjected, "You have cut the painter!" "No," said the great Bishop, turning to the speaker, " we have not cut the painter ; it has parted of itself, and we are occupied now in forging a better cable ;—like that invisible and immaterial bond by which the planets are anchored to the sun ;—We are declaring, one and all, that we have not any wish to change or alter the Articles and Formularies of our Mother Church."*

We may indeed be shown to have built a stone here and there into our rising walls less wisely than could have been wished. If so, let us, when the fitting moment comes, lay heads and hearts together to dress it into shape, or substitute a better for it. The reputation of our Chief Justice, as an upright

---

* Life of Bishop Selwyn, Vol. II., p. 235.

Judge, is not so slender as that he cannot well afford to be told that he has in some respects misunderstood us, and our position. We can equally well afford to do again, what we have cheerfully done before,—frankly acknowledge, and dutifully repair, any mistake which competent authority may finally declare us to have made in mixed matters affecting our relation to the law of the land.

APPENDIX.

[A.]

The Ecclesiastical Judgment.

SUPREME COURT.

Thursday, August 26th, 1880.

MERRIMAN *vs.* WILLIAMS.

The Chief Justice delivered Judgment in this case as follows :—

This is a suit instituted by the Right Reverend Bishop Merriman against the Very Reverend Dean Williams, praying for a declaration of the plaintiff's rights as Bishop of Grahamstown, in respect of the Church of S. George in that city, and for an interdict to restrain the defendant from interfering with those rights, and from hereafter performing any ecclesiastical functions in the said Church or elsewhere within the limits of the Diocese of Grahamstown. The grounds of action are fully, if not distinctly, stated in the declaration, and may be thus briefly summarised: that the Diocese of Grahamstown was established by Royal Letters Patent in November, 1853; that the plaintiff as the Bishop of Grahamstown is lawfully invested with the indelible characteristics of the Episcopate, and possesses a legal *status* as such Bishop, save as to coercive jurisdiction; that under the said letters patent, the Church of S. George, in the city of Grahamstown, was declared to be the Cathedral Church and See of the then Bishop of Grahamstown and his successors in office; that the plaintiff as Bishop has the right, and, until prevented by the defendant, has exercised the right of officiating and performing all ecclesiastical functions within the said Church; that the defendant having been nominated Colonial Chaplain at Grahamstown, did, on the 20th October, 1865, take and subscribe the oath of Canonical Obedience to the then Bishop and his successors in office, and bind himself to submit to the rules and regulations of the Diocesan Synod of Grahamstown in all things not contrary to the laws of the then United Church of England and Ireland; that thereafter the defendant entered upon the functions of Dean of the said

Cathedral Church; that the defendant has expressly and by implication subjected himself to certain rules and regulations framed by the Provincial Synod of the Church of the Province of South Africa for enforcing discipline in the said Church; that by the Canons of the said Church the Diocesan Court of Grahamstown is a tribunal competent to determine whether the rules of the said Church have been violated by any of the Clergy of the Diocese of Grahamstown or not, and what will be the consequence of such violation; that the defendant has been duly tried before such a tribunal for disobedience of a lawful injunction conveyed to him not to hinder the Bishop from preaching in the said Cathedral on the 27th April, 1879; that by sentences passed upon the defendant by the said Court on the 5th of August and 13th of November respectively, he was suspended from his office of Priest with total loss of all emoluments derived from any office held by him as dignitary or Priest of the said Church within the Diocese of Grahamstown; and that, inasmuch as the defendant has neither submitted himself to the sentences, nor appealed to the Appellate Court provided for by the Canons, the plaintiff is now entitled to obtain from this Court a judgment which shall enforce the sentences of the ecclesiastical tribunal and declare the rights of the plaintiff and defendant respectively in respect of the said Cathedral. The defendant does not deny that the plaintiff is a duly consecrated Bishop of the Province of South Africa, nor does he deny that the Church of S. George is the Cathedral Church of the Diocese of Grahamstown, but he contends that the plaintiff is not the Bishop of Grahamstown in terms of the letters patent, which established the Bishopric; that the tranfer deeds of the land upon which the Church stands do not support the plaintiff's title, and that his claims are inconsistent with the provisions of certain public colonial statutes. In the next place the defendant denies that he has submitted himself to the Canons of the Church of South Africa, but maintains that even if he had so submitted himself no tribunal constituted under those Canons could lawfully deprive him of his incumbency as Rector, nd of the Deanery, which he held independently of that Church; and, lastly, he contends that, even if the tribunal which sentenced him possessed the powers which it claimed and purported to exercise, yet, inasmuch as that tribunal was not properly constituted in terms of the Canons themselves, this Court ought not to give effect to its decrees. It is to be regretted that the pleadings are not so framed as to raise more distinctly than they do the real issues which the Court has to decide. The declaration, relying wholly upon the sentences of the Diocesan Court, prays not only for an enforcement of those sentences, but also for a declaration of the rights of the parties in respect of the Cathedral quite independently of those sentences, and the pleas do not merely traverse the rights claimed by the plaintiff under the sentences, but they put in issue every other right claimed by him. It is sufficiently clear, however, from the pleadings, if taken in connection with the facts disclosed in the evidence and with the argument of counsel, that the real subject of contention between the parties is not the ecclesiastical *status* in the abstract of either party, nor their personal relation towards each other, but the legal *status* of the plaintiff as well as the defendant in respect of the Cathedral Church of Grahamstown, under as well as independently of the decisions of the Diocesan Tribunal. It will be necessary then for the Court, in order to arrive at a satisfactory determination in this case, to consider, first, what are the rights of the plaintiff as a Bishop of the Church of the Province of South Africa, in relation to the Church of S. George. In the second place, what are rights of the defendant in respect of the same Church as Rector and Dean. Thirdly, whether the defendant, by his acts or conduct, has conferred on the plaintiff any rights capable of being enforced in this action, which but for such acts or conduct the plaintiff would not have enjoyed. Fourthly, whether, the respective rights of the parties are in any way affected by the decisions of the Diocesan Court. And, lastly, whether this Court, having regard to the form of the pleadings, to the facts disclosed, and the rights ascertained in this case, and to the established practice of this Court, can give the plaintiff any portion of the relief he asks for in his declaration.

I. WHAT ARE THE PLAINTIFF'S RIGHTS AS A BISHOP OF THE CHURCH OF THE PROVINCE OF SOUTH AFRICA?

Before considering these questions, it will be convenient that I should briefly state the facts which led to the present unfortunate dispute. Until the year 1847, there existed no provision for the performance within this Colony of Episcopal functions by Bishops of the Church of England, but a clause was usually inserted in the Governor's Commission giving him "the power of collating to benefices, granting licenses for marriage and probates of wills, commonly called the Office of Ordinary." Colonial Chaplains appointed by the Imperial Government, and, in most cases, ordained by the Bishop of London, under the Imperial Act 59 Geo. III., c. 60, ministered to the spiritual wants of members of the Church of England residing in garrison towns, and in a few other towns in which no troops were stationed. Among the parishes for which a Colonial Chaplain was thus appointed was that of Grahamstown, which was also a garrison town. The Colonial Chaplain was always attached to and officiated in the Church of S. George. The site on which the Church stood belonged to the Crown, but by Ordinance No. 2 of 1839 the administration and management of all matters connected with that Church were entrusted to a Select Vestry, and two Churchwardens elected under the provisions of that Ordinance. As the Clergy and members of the Church of England in this Colony increased in number, the want of Episcopal superintendence was more and more felt, until, in the year 1847, the Colony and its dependencies were by letters patent under the Great Seal constituted a Bishop's See and Diocese, and the Reverend R. Gray was thereby appointed, and was subsequently consecrated by the Archbishop of Canterbury as such Bishop. In June, 1849, and again in November, 1850, grants of the land on which the Church stood and the neighbouring premises were made by the Crown to the Right Reverend Bishop Gray upon the conditions which I shall afterwards mention. In 1853, Bishop Gray resigned the office and dignity of Bishop of Capetown, whereupon the original Diocese of Capetown was divided by the Crown into three distinct and separate Dioceses, viz., those of Capetown, Grahamstown, and Natal On the 23rd November, 1853 (before the issue of fresh letters patent to the Bishop of Capetown), letters patent were issued erecting and constituting the See and Diocese of Grahamstown, and directing the Archbishop of Canterbury to ordain and consecrate the Rev. John Armstrong to be Bishop of the said See and Diocese. The terms of these letters patent, so far as they affect the present case, will hereafter be referred to. Bishop Armstrong was duly consecrated, and shortly afterwards took possession of his See. On the 30th July, 1860, the Act No. 30 of 1860 was passed, authorising the Bishop of Capetown to transfer to the Bishop of Grahamstown any of the lands then vested in the former and his successors, but situate within the Diocese of Grahamstown, subject to the trusts mentioned in the grant; that is to say, that the land thereby granted should for ever thereafter be used for ecclesiastical purposes in connection with the Church of England, and for no other purpose. In 1863 the first Diocesan Synod of Grahamstown was held, and in 1865 the defendant was appointed to the offices of Rector of S. George's Church, and Dean, in the manner I shall hereafter explain. In 1870 the first Provincial Synod was held, and to the Constitution, Canons, and Resolutions I shall frequently have to refer. On the first June, 1871, Bishop Cotterill, by his power of attorney, authorised the transfer of the land in question to the Right Rev. Bishop Cotterill, Bishop of Grahamstown, or the Bishop of Grahamstown for the time being, the Venerable Archdeacon White, Archdeacon of Grahamstown, or the Archdeacon for the time being, the Registrar of the Diocese, and the Treasurer of the Board for the Endowment Fund of the See of Grahamstown, subject to the trusts mentioned in the previous transfer deeds, and on the 17th June transfer was passed accordingly. In the same year Bishop Cotterill resigned his office and dignity as Bishop of Grahamstown, and on the 21st of July the then Bishop of Capetown issued a mandate addressed to the defendant, authorising and commanding the Clergy and Laity of the vacant Diocese who may be entitled to vote in terms of Canon 3 of the Church of the Province of South Africa to proceed to the election of Bishop. In obedience to the mandate, the defendant sent a circular to the Clergy and Lay Representatives of the Diocese of Grahamstown, appointing a time and place for a meeting to elect a Bishop of Grahamstown. At the meeting, over which the defendant presided, the plaintiff was elected Bishop, and he was thereafter duly consecrated as such Bishop. From that time until 1875 no public dispute appears to have arisen between the parties; but in October of that year the defendant first publicly announced his intention of retiring from his connection with the Church of the Province of South Africa. He had been directed to notify in the Cathedral that a Provincial Synod would be held in Capetown on the 25th January, 1876, and he now gave the required notice, but at the same time read his own protest to the effect that such notice was given by him without prejudice to the Cathedral or to the rights and position of members of the Church of England in this Colony. The Provincial Synod was accordingly held, but defendant did not attend. From that time until December, 1878, disputes of various kinds arose between the plaintiff and defendant, the chief subject of the contention being the right of the plaintiff to preach at his option in the Cathedral. Matters were brought to a crisis in April, 1879. On the 25th of that month the Registrar of the Diocese addressed an official letter to the defendant, formally admonishing him not to hinder the plaintiff from preaching on the following Sunday. On that day the plaintiff attended the Cathedral with the object of preaching the sermon, but instead of giving out a hymn according to custom, immediately before the sermon, the Dean gave out the text of his sermon and began to preach. The plaintiff protested against the defendant's conduct and left the Cathedral. Articles of presentment were thereupon presented against him at the instance of Archdeacon White, charging him with several ecclesiastical offences, the chief of which was that of contumaciously and contemptuously disobeying a lawful requisition not to hinder or prevent the plaintiff from preaching in the Cathedral. A Diocesan Court was thereupon held under the circumstances, which I shall have to explain more fully hereafter, the defendant was found guilty of contumacious disobedience, and of conduct giving just cause of scandal to the Church, and was sentenced to be suspended from his ministerial functions for the term of one month, and, further, until he should engage not to repeat the offence. He refused to desist from performing his ministerial functions, or to give the engagement required of him, and accordingly, at a subsequent meeting of the Diocesan Court, over which the plaintiff himself presided, sentence was passed on the defendant, excommunicating him from the Church of South Africa. The defendant continued to officiate in the Cathedral, and the present action was the consequence.

THE LETTERS PATENT.

Such being the facts of the case, the first question which naturally arises is, What title do they establish in the plaintiff either as Bishop or as Trustee, or in any other capacity in respect of the Church of S. George ? For an answer to this question we are referred by the plaintiff himself, in his declaration, to the letters patent which founded the Bishopric of Grahamstown. Those letters patent undoubtedly ordain and constitute the City of Grahamstown to be a Bishop's See, and the Church of S. George to be the Cathedral Church and See of Bishop Armstrong and his successors, Bishops of Grahamstown. The subsequent letters patent to Bishop Cotterill are in precisely similar terms. If therefore the plaintiff can show that he is, under the letters patent, the successor of the first and second Bishop of Grahamstown, he will, as of course, be entitled to all the rights and privileges which they enjoyed in respect of the Cathedral Church. If the right of access for the purpose of preaching and performing episcopal functions within the Cathedral without or even against the consent of the defendant, is included amongst those privileges, the Court will be bound, in a suit properly instituted for the purpose, to enforce such right against the defendant or any other person interfering therewith. It becomes important therefore to ascertain what provisions are made by both the letters patent for the continued existence of the corporation after the death or resignation of the Bishops thereby nominated, or, in other words, in what manner and by what process their successors are to be appointed. Upon this point the terms of the letters patent are clear and unambiguous. "We do by these presents expressly declare that the said Bishop of Grahamstown, and also his successors, having been respectively by us, our heirs and successors, named and appointed, and by the Archbishop of Canterbury canonically ordained and consecrated, according to the form of the United Church of England and Ireland, may perform all the functions peculiar and appropriate to the office of Bishop within the said Diocese of Grahamstown." Now, it is admitted that the plaintiff has neither been named and appointed by the Crown, nor ordained and consecrated by the Archbishop of Canterbury; but it is argued that, inasmuch as the Crown had, before the election and consecration of the plaintiff, discontinued the practice of issuing letters patent for the appointment of Bishops in Colonies possessing Representative Institutions, the vacancy caused by resignation of Bishop Cotterill could only be filled by means of a local election and consecration. This argument affords a very good ground for respectfully requesting the Crown to appoint a Bishop for Grahamstown, and issue a license for his consecration by the Archbishop of Canterbury, but it does not in any way strengthen the plaintiff's title under the letters patent. No such application seems to have been made to the Crown by the authorities of the Church of South Africa, nor do I see how it could have been made consistently with the Canons of that Church, even assuming that the Crown would be willing to accede to the request. It has been assumed throughout the argument that the Crown would not accede to such a request, but it is by no means clear to me that the Crown has ever declared its irrevocable intention no longer to appoint Bishops for this Colony. It may well be that the Crown will not hereafter issue letters patent for the establishment of new Bishoprics in Colonies possessing Representative Institutions, but it does not follow that the Crown would refuse, upon representation made from the proper quarter, to nominate successors to Bishops appointed under letters patent which reserve this power to the Crown. At all events there is nothing in law to prevent the Crown even now at the eleventh hour from naming and appointing some other person than the plaintiff to be the Bishop of Grahamstown, and if a person so appointed were ordained and consecrated by the Archbishop of Canterbury, his title in respect of the Cathedral—so far as the existing letters patent are concerned,—would be complete. The plaintiff does not deny the right of the Crown to create the body corporate, known as the Lord Bishop of Grahamstown, and to constitute him and his successors to be a perpetual corporation; but if the letters patent were valid to create a perpetual corporation, they must have been equally valid to regulate the course of succession. The power of the Crown to ordain the Church of S. George to be the Cathedral Church and See of the Bishop of Grahamstown has been questioned, but I take it that the decision of the Judicial Committee of the Privy Council in the case of *Bishop of Capetown* vs. *Bishop of Natal* (6 Moore, P.C., N.S., 210), is conclusive on this point. That case has an important bearing upon other parts of this case, as I shall presently proceed to show. The question which then arose was whether the effect of a certain grant made by the Crown to the Bishop of Capetown, in 1850, and certain letters patent which founded the Bishopric of Natal, in 1853, was to give the Bishop of Natal the right of access to S. Peter's Church in Petermaritzburg, and the right to perform there all the services which are or ought to be performed by a Bishop in a Cathedral. It appeared that in 1850 the land had been granted to the then Bishop of Capetown "and his successors of the said See, in trust for the English Church at Petermaritzburg, and with power and authority to possess the same in perpetuity; subject, however, to all such duties and regulations as either are already, or shall in future, be established, with regard to such lands." The letters patent to the Bishop of Natal were issued at the same time, and were in the same terms as the letters patent now under consideration. Lord Justice Gifford, in delivering the Judgment of the Privy Council, after referring to the three previous cases of *Long* vs. *Bishop of Capetown*, in re *Bishop of Natal* and *Bishop of Natal* vs. *Gladstone*, proceeded thus :—"Their Lordships think it sufficient for them to say that the following propositions are not at variance with any conclusions which have been arrived at in any one of these cases, have scarcely been disputed, and cannot be successfully controverted, viz., that the letters patent were not wholly void; that there was, by virtue of the defendant's letters patent of 1847, a corporation as such capable of taking under the grant; that there was a valid resignation by the defendant (the Bishop of Capetown) of the office held under the letters patent of 1847; and that by the two letters patent 1853, of which the plaintiff's (the Bishop of Natal's) was the earlier, there was a creation of two new corporations, both capable of taking under a grant from the Crown, but neither coming within the terms of the grant of 1850, and, consequently, not taking an estate under it. The defendant's second patent, if the terms at the end of it be looked to, plainly creates a new corporation. A corporation to be capable of taking an estate under the grant alone must be the corporation described in it, and have existed at its date. Having regard to these propositions, and to the terms of the grant of 1850, be it remembered, a grant from the Crown 'subject to all such duties and regulations as are or shall be established with regard to such lands;' having regard to the fact of Natal being separate from the Cape, to the circumstances and state of the Colony of Natal, and the inception of the Church there, we consider that it was competent for the Crown, in the words of the letters patent of 1853, to 'ordain and declare that the Church in the said City of Pietermaritzburg shall henceforth be the Cathedral Church and See of the said William Colenso and his successors, Bishops of Natal,' and this being so, that the effect of the grant and the plaintiff's letters patent of 1853, was at least, to give the plaintiff the right of access to the Church, the right to officiate there as Bishop, and the right to perform there all the religious services which are or ought to be performed by a Bishop in a Cathedral, consistently with the laws and usages of the Church of England so far as the same are applicable to the Church and Colony in question. Their Lordships, founding their Judgment on all these considerations, and having regard also to the former decisions of this committee in the matter of the Bishop of Natal, do not hesitate to state with respect to the defendant, the appellant here, that he had, and has no estate or title as trustee or otherwise, and no right to interfere." With the exception of the circumstance (which does not affect this case) that the districts comprised in the Diocese of Grahamstown are not separate (as Natal is) from the Cape of Good Hope, all the remarks made by the Privy Council in regard to the See of Natal are applicable *mutatis mutandis* to that of Grahamstown as it existed at the time of Bishop Cotterill's appointment. The grants of the site of the Church and Deanery of Grahamstown made by the Crown to the Bishop of Capetown in 1849 and 1850 are almost identical in their terms with the grant of the site of S. Peter's in Natal, in 1850; the only difference being that in the grants of 1849 the terms employed to create the trust are "the land hereby granted shall for ever hereafter be used for ecclesiastical purposes in connection with the Church of England and for no other purpose or use whatever," and the grant of 1850 "the land hereby granted shall be appropriated for ever hereafter for ecclesiastical purposes in connection with the Church of England," instead of the words used in the Natal grant, "in trust for the English Church at Pietermaritzburg." The decision of the Privy Council is therefore a clear authority for the view that, by virtue of the grants to the Bishop of Capetown and the letters patent issued to Bishop Cotterill, the latter had the right before 1863 to officiate in the Church of S. George's as Bishop, and, inferentially, it is an authority for the position that, but for his letters patent, he would have possessed no such right without the consent of the Incumbent. In the year 1863 the land was transferred to Bishop Cotterill and his successors in office, with the proviso that the land so transferred should be subject to the same trust in all respects after such transfer as it was subject to at the time of such transfer. The insertion of this proviso was required by the 1st Section of Act 30 of 1860. That Act was passed, as the preamble states, in consequence of doubts which existed whether alienation of Church property could be legally made by the Bishops of Capetown and Grahamstown. These doubts arose, not as to the validity of the letters patent of the then Bishops (for the Act recognised them as Bishops, and as being capable of having legal successors), but as to the power of ecclesiastical corporations to alienate land, except for good cause shown, and with certain cumbrous formalities. Upon this point I need do no more than refer to Mulenbruch's Doctrina Pandectarum, Section 201 :—" Rerum ad pia corpora spectantium alienatio fieri non potest, nisi certis ex causis certisque adhibitis solemnitatibus." At that time it was assumed that the Bishop of Capetown, notwithstanding his resignation of the office held under the letters patent of 1847, had a legal estate in land granted to him in his corporate capacity, after his resignation and before his appointment under the second letters patent. That estate he transferred to Bishop Cotterill and his successors in office. After such transfer, Bishop Cotterill possessed, in addition to the rights which I have already mentioned as vested in him before 1863, an estate in the land recognised and sanctioned by the Legislature of this Colony. That title he could lawfully alienate under the provisions of Act 30 of 1860, or he might transmit it to his successors. In 1871 he transferred the land to the Bishop of Grahamstown for the time being and certain other parties mentioned in the transfer. The defendant denies the validity of the transfer, on the ground that the requisite consent was not obtained ; but so long as the transfer, which is a judicial act, stands registered in the Deeds Office, it must be assumed to be valid until judicially set aside. The more important question upon this point of the case is, Who is meant by the " Bishop of Grahamstown for the time being ?" Here again we can only look at the letters patent—the Charter of Incorporation, if I may so call it—of Bishop Cotterill, and we find that none can be his successor as Bishop of Grahamstown, unless nominated by the Crown, and consecrated by the Archbishop of Canterbury. Clearly, therefore, the plaintiff has established no estate or title under the transfer of 1871.

BISHOP MERRIMAN A SEPARATIST FROM THE CHURCH OF ENGLAND.

But a stronger and at the same time less technical objection to the plaintiff's title in respect of the Church of S. George still remains to be considered. That Church was founded by and for the members of the Church of England. The grant of the land upon which it stood was made by the Crown to the late Bishop of Capetown, upon the distinct trust that it should for ever thereafter be used for ecclesiastical purposes in connection with the Church of England, and for no other purpose or use whatever. But over and above the private trusts attaching to the Church by virtue of its first foundation, and of the conditions imposed by the Crown, the Statute Law of the land imposes upon those who have the custody of the Church and the administration of its affairs the obligation to hold it in trust for the members of the Church of England in Grahamstown. The 25th Section of Ordinance No. 2 of 1839 enacts that "this Ordinance shall be deemed and taken to be a public Ordinance, and shall be judicially taken notice of by all judges, magistrates, and others without being specially pleaded." The preamble recites that "it is expedient that the inhabitants of Grahamstown, and the parochial limits thereof, being members of and holding communion with the United Church of England and Ireland, as by law established, should be invested with the right and privilege of choosing and appointing, under certain regulations, a Vestry and Churchwardens for the better and more effectual administration and management of all matters connected with the Church of Grahamstown, called S. George's Church ; and that the said Vestry and Churchwardens, after having been duly appointed, should possess certain powers and perform certain duties as the same are usually possessed and exercised by such officers, according to the customs and usages of the said United Church of England and Ireland." In the body of the Act full effect is given to the objects of the Act as recited in the preamble. Only male inhabitants of Grahamstown, who are members of, and hold communion with, such United Church, are entitled to elect a Vestry, or to be elected as Vestrymen. By the 8th Section the Vestrymen are authorised to adopt or rescind such rules as may to them appear expedient for their guidance in the discharge of their duties, " and also to make such order for the management of the said Church as shall to them seem expedient," but they are expressly forbidden from framing any rules which shall be repugnant to the customs and usages of the United Church of England and Ireland. The 16th Section enjoins the Churchwardens and the officiating Minister, for the time being, faithfully to administer money contributed for charitable or religious purposes connected with the said Church and Congregation, or to "see that they be faithfully administered and appropriated in the manner and for the purposes contemplated and intended by the persons contributing to the same." The 19th Section—clearly having in view the spiritual wants of civil and military authorities, soldiers and poor people resident in Grahamstown, who are members of the Church of England—enacts that there shall be set apart certain pews for the use of the chief civil and military authorities and officers of the garrison, and an adequate number of free sittings for the use of the troops, and the accommodation of poor people. The 22nd Section enacts that the burials of all persons, according to the rites and ceremonies of the Church of England, shall take place in ground consecrated and allotted to the said Church for that purpose. An objection to the application of this Ordinance, in the present case, has been raised on the ground that the Church of England and Ireland no longer exists, inasmuch as the Church of Ireland has been disestablished, and the union between the two Churches dissolved, by an Act of the Imperial Parliament (32 and 33 Vict. c. 42), but it is a sufficient answer to this objection to say that by the same Act it is provided that enactments relating to the said United Church shall be read distributively in respect of the Church of England and the Church of Ireland. The 22nd Section of the Ordinance mentions the Church of England alone, and the Ordinance, taken as a whole, sanctions, and by implication directs the setting apart of S. George's Church for the religious worship of members of the Church of England, under the spiritual guidance of Ministers of the Church of England, and according to the laws and usages of the Church of England, so far as they are applicable in this Colony. Any doubts which might still remain on this matter are removed by the provisions of Act 30 of 1860. The first Section of that Act, sanctioning and continuing as it does the terms of the trust created by the grants made by the Crown to the Bishop of Capetown, amounts to a distinct legislative provision that the Church shall be used for ecclesiastical purposes in connection with the Church of England, and for no other purpose or use whatever. It is too late to contend, as has been done in the present case, that no legal identity can exist between the Church of England in South Africa and the Church of England in the Mother Country. That identity has been recognised by the two Colonial Statutes just mentioned, and by the decisions of the Privy Council in the cases already quoted, and of the Master of the Rolls, in the case of the *Bishop of Natal* vs.

Gladstone (3 L. L. Eq. p. 1). In England, no doubt, it is an Established Church, with all the rights and responsibilities of an Established Church; in this Colony it is a voluntary society, constituted and subsisting by mutual agreement. It follows that the Church of England in South Africa is not governed by those rules and laws which are inapplicable here by reason of their being confined to the limits of England, or by reason of their being only applicable to an Established Church, but it does not follow that the two Churches are separate and distinct. In the case of *Long* vs. *Bishop of Capetown*, the Judgment of the Supreme Court, as well as that of the Privy Council, were based upon the assumption that the Church of England in this Colony, over which Dr. Gray then presided as Bishop, was a portion of the Church of England. " We think," said Lord Kingsdown, in delivering the Judgment of the Privy Council, " that the acts of Mr. Long must be construed with reference to the position in which he stood as a Clergyman of the Church of England towards a lawfully-appointed Bishop of that Church, and to the authority known to belong to that office in England; and we are of opinion that, by the taking the oath of Canonical Obedience to his Lordship, and accepting from him a licence to officiate, and have the cure of souls within the parish of Mowbray . . . . Mr. Long did voluntarily submit himself to authority of the Bishop to such an extent as to enable the Bishop to deprive him of his benefice for any lawful cause, that is, for such cause as (having regard to any differences which may arise from the circumstances of the Colony) would authorise the deprivation of a Clergyman by his Bishop in England. We adopt the language of Mr. Justice Watermeyer, that, for the purpose of the contract between the plaintiff and defendant, we are to take them as having contracted that the laws of the Church of England shall, though only so far as applicable here, govern both." Lord Romilly, in the case of *Bishop of Natal* vs. *Gladstone*, comments, with approval upon the Judgment of the Privy Council, and after a full discussion of this and other decisions, arrives at the following conclusions: —" Where there is no State religion established by the Legislature in any Colony, and in such a Colony is found a number of persons who are members of the Church of England, and who establish a Church there with the doctrines, rites, and ordinances of the Church of England, it is a part of the Church of England, and the members of it are, by implied agreement, bound by all its laws. In other words, the association is bound by the doctrines, rites, rules, and ordinances of the Church of England, except so far as any Statutes may exists which (though relating to this subject)' are confined in their operation to the limits of the United

Kingdom of England and Ireland. Accordingly, upon reference to the civil tribunal, in the event of any resistance to the order of the Bishop in any such Colony, the Court would have to inquire not what were the peculiar opinions of the persons associated together in the Colony as members of the Church of England, but what were the discipline and doctrines of the Church of England itself, obedience to which doctrines and discipline the Court would have to enforce." We may take it then to be reasonably clear that under certain public Statutes of this Colony, as well as under the title deeds affecting the property, the claims of all persons who assert any ecclesiastical rights in respect of S. George's Church, Grahamstown, must be decided according to the laws of the Church of England, so far as they are applicable here, and I proceed to inquire how far the plaintiff's claims are recognised by, or consistent with, those laws. It is not alleged on his behalf that he is a Bishop of the Church of England, but it is contended that by virtue of his election and consecration he "is lawfully invested with the indelible characteristics of the Episcopate," and that as Bishop, "he has the right of officiating and performing all ecclesiastical functions within the said Cathedral Church." It is clear, however, that his episcopal capacity alone would not confer upon him this right, and we are therefore bound to ascertain by what religious body he was appointed and consecrated as Bishop, and entrusted with the charge of the Diocese of Grahamstown. That religious body is admitted to be the Church of the Province of South Africa. If that body is a part or branch of the Church of England, and as such entitled to appoint Bishops of Dioceses of the Church of England in South Africa, this Court would be bound to recognise its rights as against all members of the Church of England in the Diocese who interfere with them. If it is not a part or branch of the Church of England, it is difficult to see upon what grounds this Court can be asked to impose its Bishop upon a congregation, consisting of members of the Church of England, in respect of a Church which the public law of the land has devoted to "Ecclesiastical purposes in connection with the Church of England." We are, therefore, forced into the inquiry whether the Church of the Province of South Africa is a part or branch, or in any way legally identical with the Church of England ; an inquiry which I, for my part, would gladly have avoided. The designation which it has assumed is of some importance, but it is not decisive upon the question. Besides, it must be borne in mind that the preliminary resolution passed by the Provincial Synod of 1870 expressly declared that the title of the "Church of the Province of South Africa" is not intended to exclude other titles (such as English or Anglican Church), but is used to express the fact that the whole Church thus exhibited is united in this provincial organisation, through which it is connected with other Churches of the Anglican Communion and with the Church of England in particular. A more important departure from the laws of, first, the Church of England, is to be found in the following proviso of the Article of the Constitution of the Church of South Africa :—" Provided that in the interpretation of the Standards and Formularies, the Church of this Province be not held to be bound by decisions, in questions of Faith and Doctrine, or in questions of discipline relating to Faith or Doctrine, other than those of its own Ecclesiastical Tribunals, or of such other Tribunal as may be accepted by the Provincial Synod as a Tribunal of Appeal." No such Tribunal of Appeal appears to have been accepted, but the 9th Clause of Canon 22 provides that " should a Spiritual Tribunal be hereafter constituted in accordance with the provisions contained in Report II. of the Lambeth Conference, or by any future General Synod of the Churches of the Anglican Communion, appeal from the sentence of the Provincial Court, in a question of Faith or Doctrine, may be carried to such Tribunal, or if three Metropolitans of the Anglican Communion unite in requiring that the case or any portion thereof shall be re-heard or reviewed, it shall be so re-heard or reviewed." It is clear, therefore, that the jurisdiction of the Queen in Council in the interpretation of the " Standards and Formularies in questions of Faith and Doctrine" is not recognised by the Church of South Africa, and as if to leave no doubt upon the matter, another Canon (the 30th) emphatically declares " that if any question should arise as to the interpretation of the Canons or Laws of this Church, or of any part thereof, the interpretation shall be governed by the general principles of Canon Law thereto applicable." Now, we are not here concerned with the advisability or otherwise of having questions of Faith and Doctrine decided by a temporal Court of the realm. It is not difficult to understand the unwillingness of the founders of the Church of South Africa, whose acts had not always met with the approval of the Judicial Committee of the Privy Council, to exclude the jurisdiction of that Court, and to establish their own Ecclesiastical Tribunals. Be that as it may, in the construction of Canons, Articles of Religion, or Formularies the Judicial Committee is guided, not by the general principles of Canon Law, but by the laws of England. In support of this statement I need only refer to one passage in the Judgment of the Privy Council in the case of *Williams vs. Bishop of Salisbury* (2 Moore P.C., No. 8., p. 424) :—" Our province is on one hand to ascertain the true construction of those articles of religion and formularies referred to in each charge according to the legal rules for the interpretation of Statutes and written instruments ; and, on the other hand, to ascertain the plain grammatical meaning of the passages which are charged as being contrary to, or inconsistent with, the doctrine of the Church, ascertained in the manner we have described." But the first article of the Constitution of the Church of the Province of South Africa contains another proviso, which may hereafter lead, if it has not already led, to a serious departure from the doctrines of the Church of England. The proviso is, " that nothing herein contained shall prevent the Church of this Province from accepting, if it shall so determine, any alterations in the formularies of the Church (other than the Creeds) which may be adopted by the Church of England or allowed by any General Synod, Council, Congress, or other assembly of the Churches of the Anglican Communion." The consequence is that no alteration in the formularies of the Church of England, other than the Creeds, will be binding upon the Church of South Africa until accepted by it ; and as to the Creeds, if any of them, such as the Athanasian Creed, should hereafter be rejected by the Mother Church, it would be impossible for the Church of South Africa, with its present Constitution, to consent to such rejection. Here again I can quite understand the unwillingness of the Church of South Africa to be bound by laws of the Imperial Parliament, in the election of the members of which they have no part ; but, on the other hand, if it desires to have all the advantages of a perfectly free and independent Church, it cannot claim to be part of the Church of England, and as such entitled as of right to the endowments devoted to that Church in this Colony. Nor can the argument of want of representation be carried too far, for even in temporal affairs the Imperial Parliament retains the power of legislating for the Colonies, none of which send representatives to that Parliament. Coming next to the appointment of Bishops, we find in the 3rd Canon elaborate rules laying down the mode of election. In none of them is any licence, mandate, or consent of the Crown or its representative in the Colony required ; in none of them is the Crown or its representative even mentioned. It was said at the bar that the Crown has refused to have anything to do with the appointment of Bishops in the Colonies, and in support of this statement a speech of a Secretary of State in the House of Commons was read ; but I am not satisfied from what has been stated, or from the speech, that the Crown would not, if the religious wants of members of the Church of England in this Colony were fully represented to it, consent to issue its mandate for election or appointment of Bishops of that Church in this Colony. As I stated before, no such representation appears to have been made ; at all events the Constitution and Canons do not allege the refusal of the Crown as a reason for excluding the coöperation of the Crown. On the contrary, if we are to judge from the 15th resolution of the Provincial Synod of 1870, the possession of letters patent by the then Bishops appears to have been considered a hindrance rather than an aid to the development of the Colonial Church, and the question appears to have been discussed whether their Sees under letters patent ought not to be resigned. The decision, which was in a qualified negative, was in the following terms :—" That this Synod, having absolute confidence in the integrity of the existing Bishops of this Province, and being assured that legal obligations are not needed to secure their obedience to Synodical Acts, constitutions, or rules, to which they have themselves been consenting parties, is of opinion that the resignation of their Sees, as held under latters patent, would, for the present, be inexpedient." Neither the Synod of 1870, nor that of 1876, was attended by the Bishop of Natal, whose Diocese lies within the Province of South Africa, as defined by the 24th Article of Constitution. That he was expressly excluded is clear from the 3rd sub-section of this article : " By the Bishops of the said Dioceses are meant the Bishops whose names are set forth in Schedule C hereto annexed, or those persons who shall hereafter hold the Bishoprics set forth in Schedule B, according to the rules prescribed by the Provincial Synod, for determining the succession and appointment to Bishoprics in this Province ; and by Bishops of this Province are meant the Bishops of the said Dioceses, and all others who are and shall be recognised as Bishops of the Province by the Provincial Synod." Among the Bishops mentioned in Schedule C is the Right Rev. William Kenneth Macrorie, Bishop of Maritzburg, and in Schedule B his Diocese is said to be that of Maritzburg or Natal, being the Colony of Natal. But it has been decided by the Supreme Court of Appeal for the Colonies, as well as by the Master of the Rolls, that Bishop Colenso is Bishop of Natal, so far as the Church of England is concerned. By what process of reasoning then can a Church, which excludes from its Communion and from its Provincial Synods a Bishop of the Church of England, having a Diocese within the Province, claim to be part and parcel of the Church of England ? The difficulty of finding an answer to this question becomes still greater when we bear in mind that instead of the lawful Bishop of Natal, the Bishop of Maritzburg, who holds no appointment from the Crown, and whose Diocese is coterminous with that of Bishop Colenso, is admitted and recognised as a member of the Provincial Synod of the Church of South Africa. Either this

Church refuses to recognise the law of the land as expounded by the Supreme Tribunal of Appeal (a supposition which I cannot for one moment entertain), or it has separated itself root and branch from the Church of England. Let me not be misunderstood upon this matter. I do not for an instant presume to find fault with the course which the Church of South Africa has pursued to secure its freedom from external control. But I do say this, that if the Church has separated itself from the Mother Church, let it not claim, as of right, endowments which have been secured for members of the Church of England by private trusts as well as by the public law of the land. Upon every principle which regulates the relations of religious bodies towards each other, the Church of South Africa seems to be separate and distinct from the Church of England, and no authority appears to me to be required in support of this view. If authority were wanting, I need only refer to the Judgment of the Master of the Rolls in the case which I have already mentioned. I know that that Judgment has been subjected to much adverse criticism in some quarters, nor am I prepared to accept every one of the *dicta* there employed, but the decision itself has not been appealed against, nor have the principles, upon which the Judgment was founded, so far as I am aware, ever been overruled. It was necessary for the Master of the Rolls to decide what was the real *status* of Bishop Colenso as a Bishop of the Church of England in Natal, and for that purpose to distinguish between the condition of the Church of England and other voluntary religious societies in Natal. "That any number of persons," he said, "if they so pleased, might, though holding the doctrines of the Church of England, reject, either wholly or in part, the discipline and government of the Church, though they preserved still the creed, faith, and doctrines of the Church of England, is unquestionable. Such an association might elect their own Bishop; they might divide the district in which they reside into Sees, and elect a Bishop for each; they might parcel the district out into parishes and appoint a minister to officiate in each parish; all this they might do, and all this would be perfectly legal, and all this would be binding on the members of the association who assented to it; as it is now in the Episcopal Church in Scotland, which is not, and by the Act of Union is prohibited from being, a part of the Church of England, and in which the Crown is prohibited from appointing or nominating any Bishop. If dissensions arose among the members of such a Church, they must have recourse to the civil tribunals; but when they did so, the question would be tried by their own rules and ordinances, which would have to be proved by the evidence in the usual manner. But this association would not be a branch of the Church of England, although it might call itself in union and full communion with it. By the law of the Church of England the Sovereign is the head of the Church ; and in substance (for the *congé d'elire* is nothing more than a form) no Bishop can be lawfully nominated or appointed except by the Sovereign, nor, as I apprehend, could any person be legally consecrated a Bishop of such Church unless by the command of the Sovereign." It will be observed that, for the purposes of the present case, it is not necessary to adopt the reasoning of Lord Romilly in its entirety, for the Constitution and Canons of the Church of South Africa contain, as I have already endeavoured to show, other and more important points of departure from the Church of England than those which have been suggested by him. And not only do these Canons depart from the general laws of the Church of England, but some of them appear to infringe upon the special laws made by the Colonial Legislature for the management of S. George's Church. Thus we find that the persons indicated by the Ordinance as parishioners are male inhabitants of Grahamstown, being members of, and holding communion with, the Church of England ; whereas under the 24th Canon " by parishioner shall be understood any person, not being under Church censure, who is on the list of communicants, or (except the Synod of the Diocese have ruled or shall rule to the contrary) who, being baptized, and not being a member of any other religious body, is an habitual worshipper in the Church or Chapel of the parish or district, in respect of which he claims to vote." Then, again, as to the churchwardens, the 25th Canon required that they shall be communicants of the age of twenty-one years and upwards, and shall be chosen by the joint consent of the minister and parishioners, whereas under the Ordinance, the churchwardens are to be chosen by the vestry out of their own number, all of them being members of the Church of England. These Canons are general in their terms, and contain nothing to exclude from their operation Churches which are required by law to have a different management. In respect of one of these Churches, situated within the limits of his Diocese, the plaintiff now claims to have his Episcopal rights declared. That claim involves the transfer of the Church from the jurisdiction of the Church of England to that of the Church of South Africa, of the congregation from the spiritual guidance of ministers of the Church of England to that of a minister who need not belong to that Church, and of the management of its temporal concerns from a Select Vestry of members of the Church of England to a vestry not necessarily consisting of members of that Church. Such a claim involves, as I have already attempted to show, a manifest illegality. In and over the religious body which has appointed the plaintiff as its chief pastor, he is a Bishop entitled to exercise the spiritual functions and consensual authority of a Bishop, and within any Church lawfully devoted to the ecclesiastical uses of that body he is entitled to perform all those Episcopal functions which appertain to his office, according to the rules and canons of that body ; but he has not, as of right, any Episcopal authority in and over the Church of England as received and accepted in this Colony, or within any Church devoted by law or by private deeds of trust to the uses of the Church of England.

II. WHAT ARE THE RIGHTS OF THE DEFENDANT IN RESPECT OF THE CATHEDRAL CHURCH AS RECTOR AND DEAN ?

Thus far I have considered the legal position of the plaintiff in regard to S. George's Church, Grahamstown. I shall now proceed to discuss the defendant's position in regard to the same Church. He received his appointment as Colonial Chaplain in connection with the Church of England from the Imperial Government upon the recommendation, it would seem, of Bishop Cotterill. He contends that this appointment vested in him, as of right, the Incumbency of S. George's, but I can find no sufficient authority for this contention. It is admitted that successive Colonial Chaplains, appointed by the Imperial Government, have officiated in that Church, and until the appointment of the defendant, have been considered as the Incumbents ; but I am not satisfied that this usage is sufficient to establish the defendant's claims. Strangely enough, there is no evidence in the present case to show by whom he was appointed Rector. He states that he took possession as Rector by accepting the keys from the Select Vestry elected under the Ordinance, and there is no evidence to disprove this statement. We may assume, however, that all parties concerned took it for granted that his appointment as Rector would, *de facto*, if not *de jure*, carry with it the Incumbency of S. George's Church. He was subsequently installed by Bishop Cotterill in consequence of a verbal promise which had been made to him by the Bishop in England that the Colonial Chaplaincy would also carry with it the dignity of Dean of the Cathedral. It has been suggested, rather than stated, in the course of the argument, that letters of institution were granted to him as Dean, but if such letters were issued, they have not been put in evidence, and neither party has given or tendered secondary evidence of their contents. We may fairly assume, however, that the dignity of the Dean would not have been conferred on the defendant if he had not taken the oath of Canonical Obedience to the Bishop of Grahamstown, and had not made the solemn declaration that he would submit to the rules and regulations of the Synod of the Diocese of Grahamstown in all things not contrary to the laws of the United Church of England and Ireland. At that time, the Bishop of the Diocese, to whom obedience was sworn, was a Bishop of the Church of England, duly appointed by the Crown, and consecratad by the Archbishop of Canterbury, and the only rules and regulations of the Synod of the Diocese in existence were those of 1863, which do not, so far as I can gather, indicate any intention of founding a Church distinct from the Church of England. On the contrary, these rules and regulations carefully guard against any such separation. In the preface of these rules and regulations, the Bishop pledges himself to act in concurrence with the Diocesan Synod " in applying to the Church of this Diocese the laws and usages of the Church of England." In the first chapter, Clergymen who are to have seats in the Synod are spoken of as Clergymen " of this branch of the United Church of England and Ireland," and Laymen, before voting for Lay Representatives, are required to declare that they are members " of the branch of the United Church of England and Ireland in this Diocese." In the 9th chapter a similar declaration is required from persons not being communicants who claim to be entitled to the rights of parishioners. And, as if to leave no room for doubt, the rules and regulations conclude with an emphatic declaration that nothing therein contained " is intended to affect or change the position of the Church in this Diocese, or the relation of its members towards the United Church of England and Ireland, and that the Church of this Diocese remains as heretofore an integral portion of the Church of England." The rules and regulations do indeed contain a provision for the election of Clerical and Lay members " in such manner as the Bishop may determine, to sit in a Provincial Synod should one be summoned before the next meeting of the Synod of the Diocese," but a provision of this nature cannot be held, in the face of the emphatic declaration just quoted, to bind every person who accepts the rules and regulations to whatever Canons might thereafter be framed by the Provincial Synod, however widely they may depart from the principles and practice of the Church of England. For the purpose of the contract between Bishop Cotterill and the defendant, " we are to take them as having contracted that the laws of the Church of England shall, as far as applicable here, govern both." It was upon this understanding that the defendant left his Cure in England, accepted the Colonial Chaplaincy from the Imperial Government, and received

G

from the the Select Vestry possession of the Church as its Incumbent, and it was upon this understanding, we are bound to assume, that the Vestry parted with the keys, and that Bishop Cotterill, on his return from England, installed the defendant as Dean of the Cathedral, with all the rights and privileges attaching to that dignity. In the view which I take of this case, it is unnecessary to inquire minutely what those rights and privileges are. The defendant seems to hold that, in his capacity as Dean, he might have prevented Bishop Cotterill from preaching in the Cathedral, and that, even if the plaintiff were a Bishop of the Church of England, presiding over the Diocese of Grahamstown, and having S. George's Church as his Cathedral, he would not be entitled to preach therein without his (the Dean's) consent. This is certainly a startling proposition in respect of a Colonial Cathedral, which has only recently been established as such, and in regard to which no express exemptions have been proved. The authorities so ably collected and so carefully laid before the Diocesan Court by Mr. Advocate (now Justice) Shippard certainly seem to point in an opposite direction, and if it were necessary for this Court to decide the question, I should be disposed to agree with the Diocesan Court, that the proposition is untenble. But it is unnecessary for me to express a decided opinion upon this point, inasmuch as I am clearly of opinion that the plaintiff does not occupy the same position relative to the Dean and the Cathedral as Bishop Cotterill did. But for the fact that the defendant has taken part in the Provincial Synod of 1870 and in the subsequent election, consecration, and recognition of the plaintiff as Bishop of the Church of South Africa, his right to resist the plaintiff's demands would, in my opinion, have been clear and indisputable.

III. HAS THE DEFENDANT, BY HIS ACTS AND CONDUCT SUBSEQUENT TO HIS APPOINTMENT, CONFERRED UPON THE PLAINTIFF THE RIGHT WHICH HE SEEKS TO ESTABLISH BY THIS ACTION?

This leads me then to the consideration of the important question whether the defendant has not, by his acts and conduct subsequent to his appointment, conferred upon the plaintiff the right which he seeks to establish in the present action. It has been contended, very forcibly and very fairly, on the plaintiff's behalf, that the defendant, having himself become a member of the Church of South Africa, having taken part in the election and consecration of the plaintiff as his Bishop, and having in various ways recognised the plaintiff's Episcopal authority in reference to the Church of S. George, is estopped from setting up the defence which his pleas disclose. He has, it is averred, " both expressly and by implication, assented and consented, and subjected himself to the rules for enforcing discipline in the said Church, and within the said Diocese of Grahamstown, by taking part in the Provincial Synod of 1870, by taking part in the Diocesan Synod of Grahamstown, and by convening an elective assembly, and presiding at the election of, and thereafter duly installing, the present Bishop of Grahamstown, in express conformity with the Canons of the said Church." Now I may state at once that this averment has been proved to my satisfaction. It is idle for the defendant to deny that he joined the Church of South Africa, and became personally subject to its Constitutions and Canons, in the face of the active part which he took in the discussions of the Provincial Synod of 1870, and in the absence of any protest against the separatist Canons adopted by that Synod. It is still more idle for him to deny that he has subjected himself personally to the Episcopal Jurisdiction of the plaintiff, according to the laws of the Church of South Africa, in the face of the documentary proof which exists of his active participation in the election of the plaintiff. At first sight, it appears to be contrary to all reason and common sense that the defendant should now be allowed to resist the plaintiff's claims, but the more I have considered what those claims really are, and what consequences they necessarily involve, the more convinced I am that the defendant is not precluded by law from resisting them, and that the objections to his so doing are more apparent than real. We are not now concerned with the question whether the Right Reverend plaintiff has been treated in this matter with that consideration, respect, and good feeling to which his years, if not his position as a Chief Pastor in the Church of South Africa, and his labours as a Missionary Bishop, have fairly entitled him. This is a Court for the enforcement of laws of the land, and not for the inculcation of Christian charity. If the defendant's contentions are sound in law, the Court is bound to give effect to them, without regard to the question whether they have been raised in a proper spirit or not. The real question is, are they legally sound ? Now it is by no means clear to me that the principles of the English law relating to estoppel are applicable to their full extent to the law of this Colony. No doubt by our law an agreement may often be implied from the acts or conduct of a person, independently of an express contract, and the Court will in all cases refuse to assist him in acting against or setting aside such implied agreement. Such an agreement may not be called with any binding legal force so as to justify the Court in enforcing it at the suit of either party, but the Court will take cognizance of it as a ground of defence to an action brought by the person whose words, acts, or conduct have raised such implied agreement. In the Roman Law sense of the term such a pact is said to be naked (*nudum*) and the rule applies: *Nuda pactio obligationem non parit sed parit exceptionem* (Dig. 2, 14, 7, § 4). Now under the Roman-Dutch Law the distinction between agreements which are a ground of action and those which only constitute a ground of defence has to a great extent been obliterated, but in the case of such an implied agreement as that which I have supposed the rule would still apply: *favorabiliores rei potius quam actores habentur* (Dig. 50, 17, 125). I may illustrate my meaning by reference to a Scotch case of appeal, decided in the House of Lords, which was not mentioned in the argument, but which I have since found, viz., the case of Cairncross *vs.* Lorimer (7 Jur., N. S., p. 149). There it appeared that in 1827 some members of a Dissenting Congregation acquired a piece of ground, upon which they built a Chapel, which was conveyed to trustees, to be held by them " in trust and for behoof of the Associate Congregation of original seceders at Carnoustie, to whom solely, and those who shall in time coming accede to them, and continue in adherence to the aforesaid original principles of the secession the said subjects shall belong." All questions of adherence to such principles were to be decided in a certain manner. The congregation continued to use the Chapel until 1852, when a large majority, including the Minister, joined another dissenting body, called the " Free Church," which was considered to hold the same doctrines. In 1856 certain members, forming part of the minority of the original congregation, instituted a suit to have it declared that the Chapel belonged to and was to be held for the use of, those only who adhered to to the original doctrines. The defendants pleaded that it was competent for the congregation to join the Free Church, and that the plaintiffs had acquiesced in the preceeding, and were now estopped from complaining. The Court of Session held that the plaintiffs had not objected in due time to the proposed amalgamation with the Free Church, and dismissed the suit. On appeal the House of Lords affirmed the decision. The terms of Lord Campbell's Judgment were perhaps more general than were required for the decision of the case, but he distinctly observed that the plaintiffs brought the action " as individuals for a personal wrong which they individually suffer from the wrongful intrusion of others." Now if a similar case had been tried in this Court the decision would probably have been the same ; firstly, on the ground mentioned by Lord Campbell *volenti non fit injuria*, and secondly, on the ground that the plaintiffs having, by their subsequent acquiescence, been parties to an implied agreement consenting to the Union with the Free Church, could not be allowed to question the validity of such Union. But supposing the minister had reverted to the original Church of seceders, I doubt if this Court would have dispossessed him at the suit of some of those who had joined the Free Church, nor is it clear that the House of Lords would have done so. Of course that case is a different one from the present, for there was nothing done inconsistent with the provisions of any statute either public or private; I mention the case rather for the purposes of illustration. Neither by the English, nor, I presume, by the Scotch law, would the doctrine of estoppel apply so as to prevent a person from denying that the acts which are supposed to operate as an estoppel are inconsistent [*sic*] with the law. Let me put an extreme case. Supposing (if such a thing were possible) the Dean and Chapter of an English Cathedral were, upon a vacancy in the See, to proceed to the election of a Bishop without a *congé d'élire* from the Crown; supposing they elected a clergyman of some church in communion with the Church of England (say the Episcopal Church of Scotland or of America) and were parties to his consecration by Bishops of the Episcopal Church of Scotland and America; supposing that for years such a Bishop is acknowledged by the Dean and the congregation as their lawful Bishop, and officiated as such in the Cathedral; supposing that disputes were to arise between the Bishop and the Dean as to the right of the former to officiate at will in the Cathedral, and an action were brought against the Dean in the proper Court to restrain him from interfering with the Bishop's ministrations, would the Dean be estopped from denying the Bishop's rights on the ground of his not being a lawful Bishop of the Church of England? I know that the suppositions involve an impossibility, and that the case would not in every respect be analogous to the one we are now considering, but it supplies a test as to the application of the doctrine of estoppel. I do not pretend to any acquaintance with the ecclesiastical law of England, but I think we may take it for granted that the Bishop would not succeed in obtaining an injunction even against the Dean personally. Under the English common law the doctrine of estoppel is subject to some important qualifications. The case of "Stratford and Morton Railway Company *vs.* Stratton" (2 B and A 518) affords an instructive illustration on this point. There the question arose whether a person who, as a member of the committee of the company, had joined in making certain calls on shares, was estopped, in a suit brought against him, from denying the legality of the calls, and the Court of Queen's Bench decided that he was not so estopped. "I agree," said Mr. Justice Parke, "to the doctrine in 'Keane *vs*. Rogers,' that a party having made admissions by which another had been led to alter his condition, is estopped from disputing their truth with respect to that person and that transaction ; but I think it does not apply here where the question raised by the party supposed to have made the admission is one, not of fact, but of law." And Mr. Justice Taunton said : " It is clear that the defendant was not estopped. It was not competent to him to dispense with the statute under which he and the rest of the committee professed to act, even for the purpose of rendering himself liable to be sued. The calls being contrary to law, it lies in his mouth to take that objection, though he was a party to their being made." Similar conclusions would, I apprehend, be arrived at under the Roman-Dutch law, although not perhaps on precisely the same grounds. But let me now consider the question at issue as one of contract rather than of estoppel. The contract between the plaintiff and defendant was either a personal one, or it was a contract involving also the rights of both parties in respect of the Church of S. George. So far as the contract was purely personal, the defendant was bound to render due obedience to the plaintiff as his Bishop in conformity with the laws of the Church of South Africa, and he became amenable to the discipline of that Church. If he had been guilty of conduct which by the laws of that Church are punished with excommunication, suspension, or deprivation, this Court will, so far as a temporal Court can do it, assist in giving effect to any sentences passed upon him by the properly constituted tribunals of that Church. But the powers of the Bishop and of such tribunals could, under such a personal contract, only affect his position as a member of the Church of South Africa, and such offices as have been conferred upon him by that Church. But it is admitted on both sides that the defendant has accepted no office or emolument from the plaintiff or from the Church of South Africa. The facts relied upon by the plaintiff as constituting a fresh compact between him and the defendant cannot affect any office which the latter held before such compact was entered into. So far as such offices are concerned, the defendant's personal submission to the rules and canons of the Church of South Africa could not call rights or interests into existence which would not otherwise exist, or preclude the defendant, at all events, after being excommunicated by the plaintiff from communion with the Church of South Africa, from falling back upon his original contract, made not with the plaintiff, nor with a corporation, of which he is the representative, but with a corporation which, although in abeyance, is not legally defunct. But it has been contended that the compact with the plaintiff was not a purely personal one, but one which also conveyed to the plaintiff certain real rights in respect of the Cathedral, including the right of summoning the Chapter and presiding therein, " of officiating " (as the proposed statutes have it), and performing all ecclesiastical functions at his own option within the Cathedral, and in case of a vacancy in the Incumbency, of appointing a Rector, who need not be a Clergyman of the Church of England but must belong to the Church of South Africa. Such a contention, if it has any meaning, involves, as I have already attempted to show, a transfer of the Church from the control and management, temporal as well as spiritual, of members of the Church of England, to those of members of the Church of South Africa, and is inconsistent with the provisions of two colonial statutes, one of which is expressly declared to be a public Ordinance. Of these statutes the parties must be presumed to have had knowledge before they entered into their alleged compact, and neither party can successfully ask for the assistance of this Court in establishing claims contrary to or inconsistent with the provisions of these statutes. In such a case the rule of the Roman law applies : *Pacta, quæ contra leges constitutionesque fiunt, nullam vim habere, indubitati juris est* (Cod. 2, 3, 6). Before quitting this part of the case, I only desire to add that there are circumstances in evidence which tend to show that the defendant's acts, which are relied upon as constituting an estoppel, or as raising a contract, were not always quite voluntary on his part. The Provincial Synod of 1870 was convened by the late Bishop of Capetown, whose title the defendant, at all events, could not dispute. He himself says that he went to the Synod with many misgivings, and he certainly never signed any declaration of adherence to the Canons. The mandate for the election of a successor to Bishop Cotterill was also issued to him by the late Metropolitan. Possibly he might then have taken up a similar position to that which had previously been taken up by Mr. Long against Bishop Gray, but he was not prepared to take this extreme step. Having obeyed the mandate, the rest of his conduct followed as a matter of course. It was not until the plaintiff claimed the right of preaching in the Cathedral at his option that any serious controversy arose between the parties, and even then the objection raised by the defendant was to the plaintiff's unqualified right of preaching, and not to his *status* as a Bishop. It is that in 1875 the defendant protested against the Cathedral and the rights of members of the Church of England being prejudiced by the acts of the Provincial Synod, but it was not until the plaintiff had passed sentence on the defendant, purporting to cast him out of the communion of the Church of South Africa, that the defendant urged his full grounds of objection.

IV. ARE THE RESPECTIVE RIGHTS OF THE PARTIES IN ANY WAY AFFECTED BY THE DECISIONS OF THE DIOCESAN COURTS?

Hitherto I have considered the questions at issue between the parties, quite irrespective of the sentences of the Diocesan Court of Grahamstown, and it only remains for me to inquire whether those sentences in any way assist the plaintiff in establishing his right to relief. A preliminary objection has been raised by the defendant to the constitution of the Court, which passed the first sentence on him. The Court consisted of the Venerable Archdeacon Badnall as the plaintiff's commissary, with the Rev. Canon Henchman, the Rev. W. Llewellyn, and the Rev. Wm. Meaden, as clerical assessors, and Mr. J. B. Currey as lay assessor. It is admitted that the articles of presentment were duly served on the defendant, together with all notices required by the Canons of the Church of the Province of South Africa. Among these notices was a notice of the constitution of the Court and of the appointment of the Presenter's Counsel. The defendant did not appear before the Court, nor did he in any way object to the constitution of the Court. The objection which has now been raised on his behalf, is that the Court was not properly constituted, inasmuch as two of the clerical assessors were not Canons of the Cathedral as required by the 21st Canon of the Church of the Province of South Africa. The Canon directs that "the Bishop shall preside in the Diocesan Court, either in person, or, if reasonably hindered, by a commissary in priests orders . . . . being assisted by two grave priests, well accounted of in the Diocese as assessors, viz., by the Dean and Archdeacon, or some of the Canons, if there be such, when the Court is held near the Cathedral Church." That Canon certainly seems to require that, failing the Dean and Archdeacon, two of the Canons shall be assessors in their stead, but the authorities of the Church, with the most laudable desire to secure an impartial trial, appointed one Canon and two other priests instead of two Canons, it being thought that the disputes which had taken place between the Canons and the defendant might possibly have prejudiced them against him. If it were necessary to decide the point, I should be disposed to hold that as the Diocesan Court really consists only of the Bishop or his commissary, the assessors being merely advisers, and as the defendant did not, as he might have done, object to the constitution of the Court, he cannot rely upon the alleged improper constitution of the Court as a defence against an action properly brought for enforcing the sentence of the Diocesan Court. The question is not free from doubt, but for the purpose of the present case, we may assume that the Court was properly constituted. And here I may say that, in reading the proceedings of that Court it is impossible not to admire the ability and candour with which the prosecution was conducted, or the judicial impartiality displayed by the tribunal itself. Its decisions, so far as they relate to the defendant's position as a Minister of the Church of South Africa, seem to be supported by the evidence. The sentence passed on the 5th August, 1879, was that the defendant " be suspended from his ministerial functions with total loss of the income attached to the office or offices held by him as Dignitary or priest of the Church of this Diocese, for the term of one calendar month from this date ; and, further, until he shall engage not to repeat the offence of preventing the Lord Bishop of this Diocese from preaching or ministering in the Cathedral Church of S. George's, Grahamstown, and thus giving just cause of scandal or offence." The defendant, however, continued to perform his ministerial functions and refused to enter into the engagement required of him, and, accordingly, on the 13th of November, 1879, the plaintiff pronounced the defendant to be excommunicated, " the sentence to take effect after fifteen days, unless he shall in the meantime submit himself to the sentence pronounced in the Diocesan Court, and shall give satisfaction by engaging to comply in future with the rules and regulations agreed on by the Synods of this Diocese and Province." Now the effect of all this is to deprive the defendant of all offices or emoluments, which he has received from the Church of South Africa, and finally to cast him out of the Communion of that Church. It is admitted that he received no such office, and is entitled to no such emolument from the Church of South Africa, and the only operative sentence remaining against him is that of excommunication, which will, of course, prevent him from officiating in any of the Churches belonging to that Church. By the first prayers of the declaration, the Court is asked to declare that the defendant is one of the Clergy of the Church of South Africa ; but such a declaration this Court is prevented from making after the sentence of excommunication passed upon the defendant, and the remaining prayers appear to me, for the reasons already stated, to be equally untenable. I have been induced to go thus fully into the case because the parties themselves were anxious to have the opinion of the Court upon the merits. Other, but less important, objections to the plaintiff's claims have suggested themselves to me, which require a passing notice. The action is mainly a declaratory one, and yet contrary to the established practice of this Court in regard to such actions, only one of several parties interested has been made defendant. It has been stated on the defendant's behalf, and not denied on the other side, that he has the support in his conduct towards the plaintiff of the Select Vestry of the Church as well as of a majority of the congregation. But besides the Select Vestry and the congregation, the trustees, and perhaps even the Crown, may have a claim to be heard in an action for a declaration of rights in respect of the Cathedral. So far as the action is not declaratory, but asks for an interdict against the defendant, the Roman-Dutch Law requires clear proof of the plaintiff's right and title before the Court can interfere in his favour (Van der Linden, p. 440 and 441). Then, again, we have the fact that the defendant is actually in possession of the Church and the rule of our law applies: *In pari causa possessor potior haberi debet* (Dig. 50, 17, 128, § 1). From whatever point of view we regard this case, the obstacles to the plaintiff's success appear to me to be insuperable. In order, however, not to debar the plaintiff from hereafter having his legal *status* declared in an action properly instituted for the purpose, I am of opinion that the Court should absolve the defendant from the instance, instead of giving Judgment absolutely in his favour. This form of Judgment will not, I trust, prevent the plaintiff from appealing against it to the Queen in Council. If the Privy Council should see its way clear to decide in the plaintiff's favour, I for my part shall not regret the result. But, whatever course may be taken in respect of this action, I feel bound to express my individual opinion as to the necessity of legislation, whether Imperial or Colonial, to regulate the relative rights of the Church of South Africa and the Church of England, in respect to their endowments under private deeds of trust, and to legalise the transfer to the Church of the Province of South Africa of property secured by the law for the uses of the Church of England, in those cases in which there has been acquiescence for a certain length of time, or where a majority of the congregation consent to the transfer. In Canada and the Colonies of Australia, their respective Legislatures have settled the rights and *status* of the respective Churches of those Provinces, and I feel confident that unless a similar course is adopted in regard to the Church of South Africa, or unless that Church is prepared to part with some of the property of which it now enjoys the use, there will never be a lasting peace within its own household. The Judgment of the Court will be absolution from the instance, with costs, for the defendant.

[B.]
Form of Congé d'élire.

"VICTORIA, by the Grace of God, &c., to our trusty and well-beloved the Dean and Chapter of our Cathedral Church of ———.

GREETING :

"Supplication having been humbly made to us on your part that whereas the aforesaid Church is now void and destitute of the solace of a Pastor . . . . We would be graciously pleased to grant you our fundatorial leave and licence to elect you another Bishop and Pastor. We being favourably inclined to your prayers in this behalf, have thought fit, by virtue of these presents, to grant you such leave and licence, requiring and commanding you, by the faith and allegiance by which you stand bound to Us, that you elect such a person for your Bishop and Pastor as may be devoted to God, and useful and faithful to Us, and Our Kingdom."

The operation of the Statute of *Præmunire*, restraining the election to the Royal nominee under certain penalties, proves the unimpaired common-law right. The Statute of *Præmunire* does not extend to South Africa, nor is it the wish of the Crown that it should. The free election of our Bishops follows, of course, *under the laws of England, so far as they are applicable*.

[C.]
Colonial Act No. 3 of 1873.

The following correspondence, &c., &c., will show the bearings of the Act above-cited on the present dispute :—

No. I. (Copy.)

GOVERNOR SIR HENRY BARKLY, K.C.B., TO ARCHDEACON BADNALL.

Government-house, Capetown,
20th September, 1873.

The Venerable Archdeacon BADNALL, D.D., Vicar-General of the Diocese of Capetown.

VENERABLE SIR,—I have the honour to transmit, for your information as Vicar-General during the vacancy of the See of Capetown, copies of a Circular Despatch and its enclosures, received by me from the Right Honourable the Secretary of State for the Colonies, in which certain queries, founded on a Bill introduced by Lord Blachford last session into the House of Lords, are propounded.

My Responsible Advisers are of opinion that there is no necessity, so far as this Colony is concerned, for Imperial legislation in regard to the future transmission of property vested in the Bishop or other office-bearers of the Church of England for Ecclesiastical purposes,—the Colonial Act No. 3 of the present year having sufficiently provided for the regulation of all property held in trust for religious associations.

I enclose a copy of that Act, and shall be glad to learn whether you coincide in thinking that its provisions are sufficient to meet all the circumstances of the position in which the Endowments of the Church of the Province of South Africa stand; and, if not, in what respect you consider those provisions inapplicable or inadequate, and requiring amendment by the Legislature of the Colony.

* * * * * * *

Requesting the early attention of yourself and other principal office-bearers in the Church of England to the subject,

I have the honour to be,
Venerable Sir,
Your faithful and obedient Servant,

(Signed)   HENRY BARKLY,
Governor.

[Enclosed in the above were (a) a copy of Lord Kimberley's Circular Despatch, stating it to be the object of Lord Blachford's Bill, "*amongst other things, to put an end to certain doubts which are entertained as to the power and manner of transmitting property which has been given in trust to or for Colonial Bishops and their successors;*" and further stating that "*the subject appears to Her Majesty's Government to be one of considerable importance.*" (b) A copy of Lord Blachford's Bill, the preamble to which mentions the fact that "*Her Majesty has in certain of Her . . . . Possessions discontinued the appointment of successors*" to Bishops nominated by letters patent, and that "*persons duly consecrated to the Office of Bishop have been accepted as successors of such Bishops by the Clergy and Laity of the Dioceses or reputed Dioceses concerned*"; and further, that "*doubts are entertained respecting the transmission of property from Bishops appointed by letters patent to Bishops so accepted as aforesaid;*" and further, that "*it is expedient that provision should be made for the transmission of such property as aforesaid.*" (c.) A copy of the Report of a Committee of Council advising Her Majesty to withhold Her assent to Bill No. 16 of 1871, passed by the Legislative Council of Natal (among other reasons), on the assumption that the present Bishop of Natal will have no successors. (d.) A copy of Act 3 of 1873 (see Memo. of Attorney-General).]

No. II. (Copy.)

GOVERNOR SIR HENRY BARKLY, K.C.B., TO THE EARL OF KIMBERLEY.

Government-house, Capetown,
4th November, 1873.

The Right Honourable the EARL OF KIMBERLEY.

MY LORD,—I have the honour to acknowledge your Lordships' Circular Despatch of the 1st August last, forwarding, for the information of my Ministers, copy of a Bill introduced last Session into the House of Lords by Lord Blachford, with a view to put an end to doubts as to the transmission of property given in trust for Colonial Bishops and their successors, and making certain inquiries in connection with that subject.

As the best mode of answering your Lordship's inquiries, I enclose (1) copy of a memorandum drawn up by the Attorney-General, and adopted by his colleagues in Executive Council, and (2) copy of a letter addressed to me by Archdeacon Badnall, as Vicar-General, during the vacancy of the Metropolitan See of Capetown, covering a report from the Registrar of the Diocese, in the views expressed in which the Archdeacon states that both himself and the Dean and Chapter concur.

It will be perceived that the Ecclesiastical authorities consulted agree with my Responsible Advisers in thinking that the Colonial Act No. 3 of the present year will sufficiently meet any difficulty likely to arise respecting property held in trust for the community they represent, and that neither of them consider it necessary or desirable that Imperial legislation for the purpose of removing doubts on this head should take place.

I may add that the Act in question (of which a copy is appended for facility of reference), though introduced and passed after the death of Bishop Gray, was rendered applicable to such property at his express instance,—special clauses having been framed by his Registrar, and approved by the then Attorney-General, Mr. Griffiths, in 1871, though subsequently fused, when the Bill was re-cast into the general provisions now quoted by Mr. De Villiers.

As the Constitutions and Canons of the Church of the Province of South Africa are alluded to in the Registrar's report, I add a copy, together with the latest account of the administration of its funds and the extent of its endowments, in order to complete the information called for by your Lordship.

I have, &c.,

(Signed) HENRY BARKLY, Governor.

No. III. (Copy.)

MEMO.

Attorney-General's Office,
4th November, 1873.

There appears to me to be no necessity, so far as this Colony is concerned, for Imperial legislation in regard to the future transmission of property vested in the Bishop or other office-bearers of the Church of England in trust for the Anglican community.

By the 3rd Section of Act No. 3 of 1873, it was provided that as often as any immovable property shall be or shall have been granted or transferred to any office-bearer or office-bearers of any association, and to the bearer or bearers of such office or offices for the time being, shall be the owner or owners in his or their capacity of such property, as fully and absolutely as if the grant or transfer of such property had been originally made to him or them, in their said capacity, by his or their own proper names.

It might be objected that the above provisions would not meet the difficulty which was raised in the case of the "Natal Bill," viz., that they could not be effectual unless Bishops should succeed each other in legal succession. This difficulty, however, will, I conceive, be met by the powers which are conferred on the Supreme Court of the Colony by the 6th and 7th sections of the same Act. By the 6th section it is enacted that as often as by death, failure to elect, or other cause, the office-bearers or trustees of any such association shall become incapable of acting in the execution of the trusts for such association it shall be lawful for any person, being a member of or interested in such association, to apply by petition to the Supreme Court for such order as he shall conceive himself entitled to, and by the 7th section the Court is authorised, after due notice to all persons interested, to appoint trustees for the time being for such association, and to direct how new trustees shall be afterwards from time to time appointed, and to make such provision, if any, as may in the particular case appear to be required for the more effectual performance by the trustees of the trusts reposed in them.

From such an order of the Supreme Court an appeal would lie to Her Majesty's Privy Council.

The 9th section of the Act provides that the trustees for the time being appointed under the provisions of the 7th section shall be the owners in trust not only of the immovable property granted or transferred for the benefit of the association, but also of all movable property belonging to such association, and shall be invested in trust with all the rights and entitled to all the claims of such association.

By the first section the term "association" is declared to comprise, inter alia, any denomination, Christian or otherwise, united for the public worship of Almighty God, and the term "office-bearers" to comprise, in regard to associations for the public worship of Almighty God, Bishops of Episcopal Churches, and generally all functionaries by whatsoever name called who hold office in any Church or denomination.

I think it advisable that a copy of the Bill and of the queries founded on it should be sent to Archdeacon Badnall as Vicar-General, and that a copy of Act No. 3 of 1873 should be forwarded to Her Majesty's Government.

(Signed)   J. H. DE VILLIERS.

[The other documents referred to in Sir Henry Barkly's letter to Lord Kimberley are necessarily omitted for brevity's sake. They may be found in Blue-Book, C.—979, 1874.]

www.ingramcontent.com/pod-product-compliance
Lightning Source LLC
Chambersburg PA
CBHW020157170426
43199CB00010B/1086